TRUMP
TROUBADOUR
NO MORE

TRUMP TROUBADOUR NO MORE

How I Lost Faith in Our President

Kraig Moss

With Dave Smitherman

ROWMAN & LITTLEFIELD
Lanham • Boulder • New York • London

All photos are from the author's private collection unless otherwise noted.

In writing this book, the author has tried to recreate events, locales, and conversations from memory. To maintain their anonymity, some names and places have been changed including identifying characteristics and details.

Although the author has made every effort to ensure that the information in this book was correct at press time, the author and publisher do not assume and hereby disclaim any liability to any party for any loss, damage, or disruption caused by errors or omissions, whether such errors or omissions result from negligence, accident, or any other cause.

Published by Rowman & Littlefield
An imprint of The Rowman & Littlefield Publishing Group, Inc.
4501 Forbes Boulevard, Suite 200, Lanham, Maryland 20706
www.rowman.com

Unit A, Whitacre Mews, 26-34 Stannary Street, London SE11 4AB

British Library Cataloguing in Publication Information Available

Library of Congress Cataloging-in-Publication Data

Names: Moss, Kraig, author. | Smitherman, Dave, author.
Title: Trump troubadour no more : how I lost faith in our president / Kraig
  Moss with Dave Smitherman.
Description: Lanham : Rowman & Littlefield, [2018] | Includes index.
Identifiers: LCCN 2018007793 (print) | LCCN 2018028009 (ebook) | ISBN
  9781538111161 (Electronic) | ISBN 9781538111154 (cloth : alk. paper)
Subjects: LCSH: Trump, Donald, 1946– | United States—Politics and
  government—2017– | Moss, Kraig.
Classification: LCC E912 (ebook) | LCC E912 .M67 2018 (print) | DDC
  973.933092—dc23
LC record available at https://lccn.loc.gov/2018007793

To Rob

CONTENTS

1

THE TRAGIC ROAD

On April 20, 2017, CNN flew me to New York City, all expenses paid. I had a swanky room at the Hudson Hotel on West 58th Street near Central Park. I was used to driving a semi-truck hauling highly flammable liquids for a living, so having a plush mattress to sleep on was a welcome change from that cramped truck bed. That night I looked out the window at the twinkling lights of the city, listened to the steady roar of traffic, and watched as throngs of people pushed their way through the darkness, guided only by the glow of neon lights. I couldn't believe so many people, just like the ones below, had been blindsided by the unrestrained candidacy of Donald Trump. To me, it was obvious that he would win, and I had fully supported him. That's why I was asked to be on television the next day.

In the morning, after a nice breakfast, I was chauffeured to the studio where I sat on a panel with five other "average citizens" who identified themselves as having voted for Donald Trump for president. I had been interviewed countless times over the past year and I knew the drill. They wanted us to mix it up, to disagree with each other, to debate the pros and cons of Trump's actions as president of the United States on this approaching milestone—his first one hundred days in office.

I wore my trademark cowboy hat, a dark pink shirt (I like to say it's a mix of Republican red and Democratic blue), and a leather vest. As the female host of the show began asking questions, I watched some of the other panelists jockeying for attention, trying to share their views, often playing to the camera and probably hoping their coworkers, family, and Facebook friends were watching their moment in the spotlight. That was fine with me. If that's what makes 'em happy, they should go for it. However, I was there for a different reason.

I was there for my son.

2

FINDING STRENGTH

In 1985, a man named Roger hired me to work at Marshland Construction in Apalachin, New York. Roger owned and operated Marshland with his son. Roger was the kind of man who would pick someone up walking along the road and give him the opportunity to work and make some money. We thought of ourselves as misfits, but Roger had a way of drawing the good qualities out of you. He didn't care what you did in the past. "Those are yesterdays, Moss. It's todays and tomorrows that we need to be concerned with," he would say. "Life's a game, Moss. We play it the best we can," and "Life's a long hard road with many bumps and turns, you got to stay strong when things get rough." Roger would say things like, "I give you an A+, Moss. That's a damn good job!" My dad never told me I did a good job, so this was a new experience for me and I responded to the positive feedback. After I had left Marshland Construction, I kept in touch with Roger and continued to enjoy his company and crazy humor every day. He taught me that working keeps a man's mind focused and away from the dark things that can creep up on you when you least expect it.

On February 4, 1991, his son died tragically in an automobile accident at the age of twenty-one. Roger tried to keep things going for a while, but eventually sold most everything including a six-thousand-square-foot home on eighty-seven acres in the Pennsylvania mountains. He and his son had worked on the house together, and being alone with those memories eventually took a toll, and Roger put the house up for auction. It brought in good money, but Roger was never the same.

I was living in California at the time and I talked with Roger on the phone regularly. We laughed at everything and shared what was going on in our lives. After his son passed away, I asked how he handled the pain and hurt. "I hate to tell you, Moss, but it never goes away." He then said, "It goes dormant in a way. It's like your mind puts it in a closet. You know it's there, and for whatever reason, your mind opens the closet and it all comes falling out at you."

Roger was the hardest worker I knew, with the exception of a mutual friend named Michele, a French-Canadian and now US citizen, who was a damn hard worker until a back injury took him out of commission. You could see that Michele would love to do the things he did before the injury, but he just couldn't keep up with that work pace anymore. He was prescribed OxyContin. Without it, his pain was just too intense. He hated that he had to rely on a pill just to get up in the morning or go to sleep at night. However, his condition was exactly why that medication was created. However, along with heroin, OxyContin and other opioids have now been sold on the black market to young people who quickly become addicted to the powerful drugs. It has taken this country in its deadly grip and destroyed the lives of so many, especially affecting working-class folks who don't have the resources to fight and treat those addictions. I know this because it happened to my own family.

I was living upstate in a small town called Owego, New York, where I had a profitable construction business and a decent life. Things were decidedly ordinary, just the way I liked it. I had my nice little house, plenty of work equipment that I had bought over the years, and a close group of friends who shared my basic morals and values. We all looked out for each other, pitched in if someone needed help, and maybe gave a small loan until payday, anything to help out a buddy. We were all just working folks trying to keep our families together and make a few dollars along the way.

My son was living with me at the time, and at twenty-four years old, he was growing into a fine young man. I was proud of him and how he had gone through a lot of challenges, like many teenagers, but finally seemed to be maturing. Since it was just the two of us, I tried to steer him in the right direction, give him guidance without being too bossy, and make sure he was on a noble path.

It made me very proud when Rob started working with me in the construction business. It was a natural fit and he was good at it, so I was happy to be able to give him this—a start at a good, honest way to make a living. It was my hope that he would eventually take the business over from his old man and keep it going. Or maybe that experience would help him figure out what he wanted to do with his life.

Admittedly, it was sometimes a little tough because we lived together and worked together. I'd try my best to make sure we left the work issues at the front door, but that didn't always happen. We were both proud men, and since we could be headstrong at times, it could be challenging, but we kept at it. We had found a niche providing foundation repair services to folks in the surrounding areas and business just kept growing. It was hard, tough, dirty work, but we were willing to do it and homeowners were happy to pay for it.

With each job, Rob would learn a little more about the business, and he even started heading the crews for me. He was good with the guys and related to them since they were closer to his age than mine. I taught my boy how to operate the tools, how to calculate the amount of concrete needed for a job, the way to lift a foundation with hydraulic jacks and steel posts, always emphasizing the dangers of this type of work. To his credit, he kept up with me and was even able to do some things that I couldn't. He was younger and his back much stronger than mine. We learned how to depend on each other and use our individual strengths to build the business and get each job completed on time, just the way I always promised the homeowners. My business was built on referrals, so my word was my bond.

As Rob took on additional responsibilities, I started teaching him more about the financial side: how to keep the books, drum up business, and collect payments. I would also go over how valuable each piece of equipment was so that he would understand what risks were involved. There was also another reason.

"Why are you telling me how much these tools are worth?" he'd ask.

"Because that's an $800 jackhammer," I said pointing to the well-used tool laying by the truck. "And if something were ever to happen to me, you'd understand what you've got here." I saw him twist up his mouth and I knew he was uncomfortable with the conversation.

"Come on, Pop, let's just go eat."

Rob quickly learned to operate the backhoe, small dozers, skid steers, stone cutters, and every power tool I owned. He was a natural and those were good times. Working with my son, we would talk about the future, joke around about our dating lives, and discuss upcoming projects. We would go four-wheeling, camping, fishing, and boating. We also liked to check out car races.

When we were a young family just starting out, I would take Rob and his two stepbrothers (my wife's sons) to the California 500 in Fontana. I'd stop by Walmart on the way to Fontana from the Fresno area and buy the biggest binoculars I could find. The three boys would use them to watch the race and then I would return them for a refund the next day. I did this with visits to the beach as well. I'd buy the nicest floats and beach chairs and just bring them back when we were done. Not the noblest thing I'd ever done, but we didn't have much money. The boys loved it and we had a great time. Being a dad was a big part of my identity and I enjoyed every phase of Rob's life, from toddler to young adult.

In 2013, Rob was making a decent salary in the foundation business. I was paying him around $17 an hour plus bonuses. He was doing better than a lot of his friends and it was good to see him handle his own money responsibly. I'm sure his girlfriend liked that too. She was a nice girl—a real cute young lady. Rob had gone through an awkward stage as a teen, and I was glad that he seemed to be coming into his own. He was working, had a decent group of friends, and now had what seemed to be a good girl to spend time with.

One night I had fallen asleep and woke to all kinds of commotion coming from the other room.

"Rob, what is going on?" I asked.

"She's out of here!" he yelled.

I looked out the window and saw clothes and things strewn across the front yard. "Rob, you can't treat her like that. What has gotten into you?"

"Dad, she's a junkie. I found a needle in her purse. She didn't want to leave, but I told her she has got to move on."

Wow, my head was spinning. That was from out of left field. I guess it's true that parents really don't understand a lot of what their kids are going through, but I had thought we were close. To have this come up unexpectedly, I was just stunned. I'd heard a little about heroin becoming popular, especially in rural, depressed areas like ours where there weren't a lot of job opportunities. From what I'd heard, the drugs were becoming much easier to get, and most kids got hooked after the first or second try. Then it was all over for them. It affected the wealthier folks, too, just in a different way, as they became hooked on opioids that were all too frequently prescribed for pain. So, I knew shit like this was going on, I just didn't think my son would be so close to it. As a parent, it scared the hell out of me.

The next day, I was going over some paperwork for the business when Rob came in through the front door of our home. "Pop, I got something to tell you."

We sat down in the living room. "Go ahead," I told him.

"I've smoked heroin before. Since I kicked my girl out, she's threatening to call and tell you about it, so I wanted to do it myself. I ain't gonna lie to you no more. I did it and I just wanted you to know."

I was completely shocked. I never figured my boy for a druggie, but I didn't want to come off too hard on him. He was a grown man after all. "Son, I commend you for your honesty, I really do, but I gotta ask you, Rob, is your life that bad? I thought things were going pretty good for us. Why would you even get near that kind of stuff? You know it is killing people. We've talked about that before."

"I know, I know. Don't worry. That's exactly why I made her leave. I did it and didn't like it. She's into it and I just can't be around that."

"Since she had that needle, I'm guessing that means she injects it or shoots it up, or whatever you call it, and you smoke it?"

"I smoked it, Pop. Not anymore. I tried it, but I have no desire to do it again. I'm done. I just wanted you to know."

As a parent, all kinds of things were running through my mind. I guess I felt a little better after he reassured me that he wasn't into it, but I started thinking about other things. I remembered there was one time when he came home from hanging out with friends and he was slurring his words. I considered myself a fairly perceptive guy, but I just thought he was drunk. I had never thought about the possibility of drugs.

Then there was another time when he came home with a bloody head. "What happened?" I asked.

"Dad, I got into a car wreck."

Things seemed to quiet down after that. In October 2013, we were working on a huge job and he was just so much fun to be around. That was exactly the way I had imagined it. We enjoyed each other's company, we got the job done, and then we went home and did our own thing. It was coming together real nice. I would make sure to take care of him and the crew. Even though we had work to do, we also had some fun. Hell, we'd go out for lunch, and if things on the job were moving along, we'd stay out for an hour and a half or so, just talking and messing around. We'd take the whole crew with us. I wanted everyone to bond and enjoy being together. I told Rob, "Life is too short to be working so much. I enjoy eating with you guys. Let's take our time. No rush."

Then later that month, I noticed on his phone that his former girlfriend was calling. "Are you back with her?" I asked as I started to feel that uneasiness creep back into my mind.

"No, I'm not, Pop. She's just checking in."

"Rob, I gotta tell you, that concerns me."

"No, don't worry. I'll take care of it."

Then he started staying out later than usual. He'd get home early in the morning and then turn around and go to work at the job site. He used to stay in during the week and read or tag along with me to scout out new job sites. Now I noticed that he was hanging with a new group of friends, and as a parent, I had some concerns about the guys I'd seen him with.

Of course, I knew that I needed to address my concerns, so I tried to approach the topic without pissing him off. "Rob, what's going on with this new crowd? I don't have a good feeling about them."

"They're my friends. I thought you always said don't judge a man by skin color, religion, or the car he drives. So, you shouldn't judge them."

"That's true, son, but I also know when something doesn't seem right. These seem like some bad guys to be around."

"Don't worry, Dad. Trust me. I'm not messing up."

The next month, our new project was in full swing. We were working on an old farmhouse that had only half a basement. The owners engaged our services to build it out to a full basement. It was a huge job and would take a few months. First, we tore the foundation walls out, jacked up the house, fired up the backhoe, and dug dirt out from around the base of the home. Then we could pour the footers and most of the wall set. It was a lot of work, but I'd done it many times before, so I knew we just had to keep everyone on schedule to get it done on time. Then I'd make sure it passed city code and get everything certified.

In December, Rob came to me with a request. "Dad, I'd like to go see Pastor Mark."

"Pastor Mark? You know we usually go in the spring." Every April, Rob and I would make our way down to Florida, to the cowboy church where we would pray, sing, and enjoy fellowship. We had some of our best times on those trips. We would ride around on golf carts with me playing my guitar and Rob flirting with the ladies. It was always a time when we could relax and get away from work. Maybe this tough basement job was getting to him more than I had realized.

"Rob, you're going to put us in a bind," I told him. "You want to go to Florida while we have a house up on stilts! You know this project will be finished in the spring, just in time for our trip. Right now, we got the sewer exposed. We have to think about those homeowners and you want to leave now? What are you thinking?" He agreed that it was probably a bad idea and went to his room.

Our goal was to get the house situated before the ground froze. As it was, we would still have to wait until spring to finish up, but the more we got done before that, the better off the project would be. So, we pushed ourselves and our crew. On Christmas Eve, the snow was coming down hard, but we kept going and finished backfilling the dirt around the base of the foundation. I was very satisfied with how much we had accomplished and realized we were at a good stopping point for that phase of the project. Plus, that meant we would get the next installment of our fee, just in time for the holidays.

Rob smiled as I gave him $3,000, which was his share of the payment we had just received. "So, are we doing anything for Christmas this year or do you just want to wing it?" I had been so focused on the job that I hadn't really thought about it. We didn't have a tree or anything and we just kept it simple.

"Here," I told him. "Take my Sears card and go get a jacket or something as your present."

"Do you want to come along?" he asked.

"No, son, I'm tired. Just take the truck."

After a little while, he returned and even brought me some socks as my gift. The next day, we went to church and had Christmas dinner with some friends. It was low key, but I was fine with that and he seemed to be as well. On New Year's Eve, I was headed off to church and Rob wanted to go out with his friends.

"Just remember, no drinking and driving," I warned him.

"I know. I'm not stupid. You taught me to never do that."

"You sure you don't want to go to church? You could help me with my sound equipment."

"No, if it's okay, I'll go out with friends and we'll even take a taxi so you can relax."

We had our plans in place, and I went to church and played my music. I got home at around 1:00 in the morning, but Rob wasn't there yet. I was sure he was still out enjoying himself and I went on to bed.

When I woke up and went to check on him, I saw that his room was empty. I got a little panicked. I looked outside and saw that my truck wasn't there. That was odd since he had taken a taxi last night. I hopped into my dump truck and headed off to find him. I got about halfway down the big hill when I saw my pickup parked on the side of the road. Then the cops came along with Rob in the backseat.

Apparently, he had returned home sometime during the night. He was drunk, but he had been taking taxis all night. Not only that, he had been paying for all his friends to ride in cabs from one party to the next. That could really add up out there in the country where getting from one place to another normally took thirty minutes one way. He had his work money and he was certainly having a good time with it.

I found out that when he had come back home last night, he'd realized he'd left his cell phone in one of the taxis. He tried calling the company, but got no answer. Then he took my truck keys and drove, drunk, to the taxi company where, miraculously, they had found his phone. On his way home, still very drunk, he stopped at a convenience store to get cigarettes. There was a cop car parked in front of the doors and the police were inside. Rob pulled up, stumbled out of the truck, and went in to buy some smokes, clearly inebriated. The cops told me that they stood stirring their coffees as they just watched and waited for him to get back in the truck and drive off.

Then one of them said to the other, "Well, I guess we got another one." They went out to their car and followed Rob, pulling him over and giving him a DWI. They were bringing him back from the station when I saw them.

After the cops left, Rob was incredibly embarrassed, but I tried to take the sting out of it since what was done was done. "It's not the end of the world," I told him. "We can get Carlos or one of the other guys to drive you if necessary. Hey, maybe you can even get one of those conditional licenses, so you can still drive to work."

"Pop, I don't want to talk about it now."

"You gotta think about what I'm going through, son. When I'm gone, everything I have is yours, but if I can't even go to sleep without wondering if my truck is going to disappear, then we got ourselves a problem." I was definitely getting worked up at that point. "You know I would have come to help or pick you up or whatever. Right this minute, I'm not sure I want you around anymore."

I realized I had probably gone too far, but that was how I felt at the time. I just couldn't believe he had put himself in jeopardy like that. Still, I went with him to see an attorney, which Rob paid with $1,500 cash from the money he still had left. He didn't want to let go of it, though. "Oh, man, that is all of my money."

The next Monday, I started a new job with Chesapeake Gas and Oil in Pennsylvania. That would allow me to have some steady work and get benefits during the winter. While things were slowing down on the farmhouse job, Rob was set to take over for me and manage the project. I thought it would be good to assign him more responsibility and hopefully it would give him something else to focus on besides his recent troubles.

I was up and ready to go at 6:00 a.m. I yelled to his room, "Rob!"

"Yeah?"

"I'm going to work now. It's your first day solo so I left $100 on the stairs for gas and lunch for the guys. Get five gallons of diesel for the backhoe, too."

"All right."

Every time we would leave each other, even if it was just to run an errand or something, we'd always add a simple "love you." But I didn't say it that morning. I was excited about this new job with insurance and benefits, and I really was eager to get started and make a good impression. Halfway through the day, I texted Rob for his social security number. His text reply was a little cocky. *Why do you need that? Hope you're not thinking about writing me off on your taxes.* I was a little surprised by his response, but assured him, *No, this is for the life insurance policy and beneficiary forms.* No response.

I got home at about 5:45 in the evening and called into the quiet house. "Rob?" Nothing. "Rob!" I waited to hear that comforting, *Yeah, Pop?* But all I got was silence. The dump truck was in the driveway, so I thought maybe he had walked into town or took a taxi because of the DWI. I was anxious to talk to him to make sure he was doing okay and ask how work went that day.

I called Carlos. "How did you guys make out today?"

"Your son is sick," Carlos said. "We quit early."

"Where is he?"

"He is home. He was much too sick to socialize. Maybe you will find him."

"Okay, thanks, Carlos. I gotta go."

I opened the door to his bedroom and the overhead light from the hallway flooded in, chasing away the darkness. I squinted for a second and then saw his silhouette on the bed. He was lying on his back, hands clasped together across his chest, eyes closed. I got a sinking feeling and rushed to his side. I shook him. "Rob! Rob!" Nothing. I checked, and he wasn't breathing. I dialed 911. "My son's not breathing. I'm starting CPR! You're on speaker phone. Now I'm giving him the chest compressions and then mouth to mouth." I performed that procedure over and over. I think I blew too hard and it got in his stomach as air came back up with a strong stench.

"What color is he?" the operator asked.

"Pale! He's definitely pale, with some purplish veins around his ear. Where is the ambulance? When will they be here?" It seemed like an eternity. I was getting tired, but I was not about to stop.

"They are coming. They are on the way."

Out of nowhere, I felt a pair of strong hands grab me and pull me away from my son. The police had arrived, and I hadn't even heard them come in. As they assessed the situation, one cop pointed to the needle beside the bed that I hadn't even noticed. I just stood there, not sure what to do. Then the EMTs came in and asked me to leave so they could get to work.

I went up the flight of steps in our split-level and sat on the sofa. I could hear everything going on. There were four officers and a lot of emergency workers. They were trying their best to revive my son, but it was no use. It felt like time was moving in slow motion, like an instant replay. Sounds were garbled, my mind was swirling. I could hear the verbal instructions coming from the defibrillator. *Open patient's airway. If there are no signs of life, remove clothing from chest and stick on electrodes . . .*

They worked on him furiously. I could tell they were frustrated. I didn't have a good feeling at all. It was at that moment that I also remembered that in October 1999, my father, Richard Moss, died in that very room. I felt a shiver run down my spine. I was just waiting for the word, for them to confirm what I already knew to be true. I heard a lot of chatter and then suddenly it all stopped. Everything was quiet for a moment. Then they came out of the room and stood at the foot of the stairs. I heard the EMT call to the police officer in the foyer, "We lost him. Gonna need a body bag."

I immediately perked up. "You are not taking him out in a body bag! My son will not go out in a body bag!"

"Sir, sit down."

"No. I'm going to him now, and when it's time, you are going to take him out on a stretcher." Then I went to my son. His shirt was open, his skin even paler than before, starting to take a grayish tone. It was him, but it wasn't. I wanted to speak to him just once more. "Rob, what happened?" I held his flimsy hand in mine. I started talking about the things we did. Everything was flooding my brain, all of the adventures we had. I didn't want to leave him, and I didn't want him to leave me.

Finally, they said it was time to take him away. I went back upstairs while they did what was necessary. I was glad that at least he was leaving on a stretcher as I had demanded. My good friend Conrad came over after he heard what had happened. We would hang out from time to time when he needed a break from the pressures of life. I was glad to have him there.

I told him about the time a few months ago when I woke up at 3:00 in the morning and felt compelled to write down some lyrics that were in my head. It had only taken about twenty minutes because it flowed out of me so organically. I began singing the words of the song, "Lord, why am I so lonely? My mom and dad have passed away, my best friend gave up on life today." Then Rob came into my room and he was irritated. "Really, Pop, you're going to get up at 3:00 in the morning to play guitar and sing?"

"I couldn't help it, son. The Lord put these words and this music in my head and I had to write it all down."

He leaned over my shoulder and started reading the words. "Who is your best friend that gave up on life?" he asked.

I said, "I don't know. I'm just writing down what came to my mind."

Then I looked at my friend Conrad. "You know, I think subconsciously I was writing about Rob and he had actually given up on life at that moment. I just didn't understand at the time that those words were about him. Now I do."

"What's the name of the song?" Conrad asked.

"Lonely."

Conrad stayed with me that night. At 6:00 the next morning, he said, "I have to go to work now. Will you be okay?"

"To be honest," I said, "I'm not really sure."

Conrad and another friend, Tom, helped me with the gut-wrenching plans regarding how to bury my son. I was no help at all. I just couldn't function. They took charge of getting him clothes. They had a suit dry-cleaned. Tom bought him a nice shirt and Conrad got a tie. They dressed him and prepared him for the service, which I appreciated. I was surprised that his mother was not in attendance, but I chose to focus on the many family and friends who did show up to celebrate Rob's life.

Right after the service, my friends presented me with the same tie that they had bought for Rob so that we would both have one. I couldn't have imagined how I would have gotten through all of that without those guys.

Months later, I kept replaying scenes in my mind. Why hadn't I taken Rob to see Pastor Mark when he asked? Why had I been so focused on work that I couldn't see when he was hurting? How could I not even understand the message of my own song? Was I overlooking the signs because I didn't want to face what was happening?

For almost two years, I was like a shell of my former self. I was lethargic, unmotivated. I just didn't have the will to go on. My construction company stopped taking new jobs. I didn't feel like I could put all my effort into it and that wasn't fair to my customers. I was grateful for the overwhelming support I received from family and friends after Rob's death. My aunts and uncles, my ex-wife Jo-an and her family helped me deal with the loss, but I just couldn't shake the constant pain.

I also noticed that I was almost emotionless. In August 2015, I lost my good friend Conrad to cancer. I couldn't even muster a tear. I was still numb from the loss of my son. Nothing that happened around me seemed to affect me anymore. It was like my emotions died when Rob did. I felt paralyzed, like my soul was being held hostage, like part of me had gone away and I wasn't sure if it would ever come back.

One day I was looking online for a cutting torch and welder to buy for my business. I came across an ad showing the exact torch I'd been looking for. I went to the address the man gave me over the phone, and when he took me into his garage, I was greeted by an eight-by-fifteen-foot painting of Donald Trump with a bald eagle clutching an American flag just before it hit the ground. It was a magnificent piece of artwork and with the size of the painting, well, I'm here to tell you it was just jaw-dropping to me. I was amazed by the power of the painting. This man was selling his possessions to fund his journey to Iowa to attend a rally for presidential candidate Donald J. Trump.

Maybe this is exactly what I needed in my life. What did I have to lose? I wanted to find a way to pay tribute to my son and hopefully shed light on this horrible drug epidemic that was sweeping our country. No one seemed interested in talking about the problem. Maybe if I could get the attention of someone important, of someone powerful, just maybe that person could help to make sure this didn't happen to anyone else.

We hit it off immediately, and after another visit with my guitar and a few performances of some of my Christian songs, he asked me if I'd be interested in joining him in Iowa for the unveiling of his Trump painting. He said I would have to provide my own transportation to and from Iowa, but I could play my Christian songs before the showing of the painting to fifty or so supporters and some media folks. I accepted the invitation. This seemed like just the thing I needed to pull me out of my slump. It was in November 2015, and January 6, 2016, would be two years since Rob died. It all seemed so divine. I knew that I needed to follow these signs, so that's exactly what I did.

After playing and singing at the Iowa event, we met a lot of great people and the artist exchanged information with many of them to keep in touch while on the Trump Trail. There was a lot of hard work involved in crating up the actual painting and loading it into the box truck that was wrapped on the outside with a copy of the painting. Oh man, what a scene at the airport when the artist came to pick me up! There were both extremes. Some people were giving a thumbs-up while others tried to ram their car into his truck, especially when they saw what was inscribed on the side: "God has chosen

Donald J. Trump for president." This didn't sit well with most folks. Even Trump's strongest supporters thought it was a little too much.

On January 15, 2016, the day after the Iowa show, we went to a rally in Urbandale, Iowa. We arrived early, and the artist initiated what he called "strategic parking," which was simply pulling the truck along the curb of the building very close to where the people would enter for the rally. He had prints of the painting and sold one now and again to fund his venture. He also had postcards of the painting that we handed out to keep interest going.

After playing some Christian songs and old country like "Jambalaya" and "King of the Road," I went inside to join the rally. Somehow, I managed to get up close to the stage. This venue was only big enough to hold maybe two thousand people. After waiting for a long time, a familiar-looking man came on stage. There he was, big as life. Donald J. Trump. The audience went wild and started chanting, "Build that wall, build that wall!" After he spoke for a few minutes, Trump asked if anybody had a question they would like to ask. I raised my hand. He pointed at me. "Yes, sir, what's your question?"

I was shocked, but quickly pulled myself together. "If you become president, what will you do to combat the ongoing heroin crisis we find ourselves in? I lost my son to heroin two years ago and I was wondering what you will do in regard to this problem."

Trump paused as he saw me break down. For some reason, my emotions took over and I was filled with pain. It was like Rob's spirit was with me. I couldn't believe someone like Trump was actually listening to a regular guy like me. It was very powerful. Trump came from behind the podium and stood at the front of the stage, towering over me. He said, "Calm down now, things will get better with this problem. Trust me. In honor of your son, we're going to fight the war on drugs. This heroin is a tough drug to kick from what I'm told. We need to make treatment facilities more available and affordable for people to get off this stuff. Your son would be proud of you." Then he turned to the crowd. "Folks, this is a good father, I can tell you right now." The audience applauded loudly, and I felt a few hands patting my back. Many people pulled me aside on the way out and told me of their lost child or brother or sister. That was all I needed to hear, all I needed to have happen to convince me I was on to something. This is what I needed to do. I had found my purpose, or maybe it had found me.

Later that evening, the artist had a political big shot come to the hotel room where we were staying. The first thing on the agenda was that the artist asked me to stay on what we called the Trump Trail with him for the entire month of January and we would campaign for Donald Trump. I had flown in with one change of underwear, one extra pair of socks, and a spare shirt. I had about $300 to my name, but he assured me that all I had to pay for was my meals. That was the deal. Just play guitar and pay for my own meals. After all that had happened at the rally, after I had spoken to the man himself, it didn't take much for me to say, "Yes, I'll do it!"

Now we had the representative in the room wanting to finance the whole thing. I thought for sure there would be some money coming our way. Mostly for the artist, but they talked earlier about getting me $350 or so a week for expenses. The man sat down with an Iowa map showing all the counties. It was all looking good. I think the compensation for the artist and his truck was about $850 per week to come from contributions to the Trump campaign, but he said he wasn't interested. I couldn't believe it. It seemed the representative was given the green light to offer compensation as long as we knew the marching orders would come from the money source. It was going to appear that the truck was the organization's idea and that they were doing this for Trump. It was still the artist's painting and truck, but it would take the spotlight away from him and focus more on the organization. I just couldn't understand his reasoning. We needed money and here it was. But because of some ego trip, he wouldn't budge, so we ended up living like paupers for the entire month of January. He promised me that he had some rooms lined up. It turned out some of those folks at the show had offered their home for a night or two while he was in Iowa. He had to get the okay for me since they had only offered the rooms in their homes to him, and the plan was that I would fly back to New York.

With a basic plan in place, and no money to speak of, we headed out to one rally after another, stopping at this house or that one for a quick rest and maybe a shower. Along the way, we prayed several times a day. The artist told me that either we pray or be prey, and I agreed. I was basically beholden to him, so we prayed about everything. I remember we received a lot of blessings in Iowa. One night we prayed for a safe trip, about 150 miles, to our next destination. The artist spoke calmly with his English accent, "Kraig, is this truck supposed to be on our side of the road? What do you suggest I do?" I looked up and saw a truck barreling right for us in our lane! I yelled at the top of my lungs, but he always remained so calm. Luckily, we avoided a collision and continued on our journey. The artist also prayed with his wife and children every night before bed using Skype. He was really a Godly man—so it would seem.

We met such wonderful people on the Trump Trail. Everyone was so trusting and loving, especially those first folks in Iowa. It really set the tone for what was to come. It felt like the two of us, this odd couple of the singer and the artist, were on a mission to spread the word about this new, renegade candidate who would surely set the world right again after the abysmal Obama years. Everyone we met on the trail felt the same way and it was infectious. I was sure that I had made the right decision by staying on the trail and continuing with our mission. I felt like I had a purpose and a real reason to get up in the morning. We were helping to make this all happen. We were a part of this great plan to "Make America Great Again." I was going to talk about my son, play the guitar, and sing my own songs while supporting the man who told me that in honor of my son he would fight the war on drugs. "Trust me," he had said. This is the man I was going to vote for, the man who would "tell it like it is."

I was on cloud nine. It seemed too good to be true.

3

LOVE LOVE LOVE

Being raised in upstate New York was almost every child's dream. I grew up in Apalachin, New York, surrounded by wooded areas, creeks, fields, and plenty of fishing spots like ponds and rivers. It was rural America at its finest and a small boy's dream come true. However, I later found out that it was so rural that the Mafia chose to hold their big meeting at Mr. and Mrs. Barbara's horse ranch on McFall Road in 1957, and it became town lore to be told and retold to this day. Both of my parents had good jobs working at IBM. Mom worked nights and Dad did the day shift. There was plenty of money, great Christmas presents, everything a kid could want, but as the old saying goes, you can't buy happiness.

My dad slept in the basement for as long as I can remember. At some point, he must have gone upstairs (or maybe my mom made a visit down there) because I got a baby sister named Cynthia Lisa Moss when I was about three years old. I was excited to have a sibling, even more so later on when we would cling to one another while the fights took place.

Fighting was a regular occurrence in our household. The fights were always about something mundane like Mom cutting the roast beef too thick, at least that's what I saw, but I suppose there were deeper issues that I was not aware of. My dad drank at the bar every night and used to tell me his buddies made fun of him for living in the basement of his own home. Every few months, he would decide that he was reclaiming his rightful place in the master bedroom upstairs only to be overruled by my mother. She had been raised in New York City until she was seventeen and she was good at standing up for herself. No one was going to push her around. Ultimately, my dad would end up whining and muttering as he made his way back downstairs to his "dungeon" as he often referred to it.

It wasn't long before Dad started taking his frustrations out on me. At age five, I remember vividly that my dad was hitting me with an adjustable wrench, but I can't remember the reason. He would pick up any nearby tool when he got angry—it could be a ⁹⁄₁₆ wrench or the wood of a screwdriver handle—and hit me on the back of the head. This particular time it was an adjustable wrench, and after the blow, a golf-ball-size knot appeared on my head. I was crying so hard that I couldn't stop myself. Every time it happened, I would be so shocked that the man I looked up to would do that to me and cause me so much pain on purpose. It was humiliating and scary for a young boy. "Oh, quit your crying!" he hissed. "I didn't hit you that hard."

All three of us were in the kitchen and I was massaging the lump on my head. Mom asked me what had happened. "Don't tell me. I already know," she said and turned to my father. "If you ever touch him like that again, I promise I will kill you myself."

It felt very uncomfortable to be in the middle of the two of them and their fighting. I loved both of my parents, despite the way they treated me. It was the only way of life that I knew and I figured that's what every kid went through. After that incident, my father did change his ways somewhat. Instead of striking me, he would ask if I wanted to talk to him. Of course I did because it made me feel like he was spending time with me. When we would get alone, he would flick his forefinger off his thumb and pop me on the head. It still hurt, but it was nowhere near as painful as those tools.

I always tried to impress my dad, but I seemed to fail in every attempt. Nothing was ever good enough. "You'd fuck up a free lunch," he would always tell me. When I joined Cub Scouts, we would occasionally make things to take home. When I'd show Dad what I'd made, he would always point out the flaws—an unsanded portion of wood, running paint, that kind of thing. It was difficult knowing that Dad would always point out flaws.

After my sister got a little older, she started to understand the dynamics in the house. One day when she was five and I was eight, Dad and Mom were fighting, and it was particularly volatile. Broken dishes, glasses, and other breakables were hurled across the room, shattering on impact. I heard my sister yell out, "Stop fighting!" I stayed in my room hoping that the incident would end soon. I heard my dad rubbing the hall walls with his shoulder for balance as he stumbled toward my room. He flung the door open and I immediately smelled the familiar odor of booze mixed with the half-smoked cancer stick dangling from his lips. He would get down on his knees in front of my bed and start talking.

These moments always made me feel uncomfortable because he would try to reassure me or tell me his side of the story, and since he was beyond drunk, he rarely made any sense. "Kraig," he said, "I'm sorry you and your sister have to hear your mom and I fight. We're trying to work things out. We're trying to work things out, you see, because you were a mistake, but we're going to keep trying for you kids. You see, mommies and daddies are supposed to sleep together."

I knew this was true because I had asked all of my friends if it was normal for parents to sleep in different places. They laughed at me and thought I was kidding around. I didn't tell them that my dad slept on a small cot with tattered *Playboy* magazines strewn around on the floor. I think he had every issue from the beginning of the magazine. He also had a pinup calendar on the pegboard over his tool bench, which was situated beside his cot. After he told me they were fighting but staying together for us, it made me feel even worse. It felt like me and my sister were the reason they fought so much.

After each argument, they would usually make a gallant effort to be "normal" only to fail and fall back into the same old patterns. One time we went camping with about six other families from our neighborhood. When we got to Selkirk Shores, Dad set up the pop-out Wheel Camper. Just as soon as we got situated, as usual, Dad took the car and went off to find a bar. When he came back to the camper that evening, he and Mom got into a huge blowout. I took my sister and walked to the Crown's campsite. "Your mom and dad fighting again, huh?" Mrs. Crown said. "Well, come over here and get a marshmallow and a stick. You kids can roast 'em with us."

The Crowns lived one house and a bridge away from us on Long Creek Road. I loved going there since they had four boys: Mick, the oldest; Jeff, who I claim to have been my best friend as a kid; and then Steve and Gregg. They were the family I wanted ours to be. Not a lot of money but just a plain old normal and loving family. Mrs. Crown was our babysitter until I was nine years old. Dad would usually show up drunk to pick us kids up and that didn't sit well with her, not to mention all the times he would miss the driveway in the winter and end up in the front yard. She was also my den mother for Cub Scouts and I often went fishing with them. Mr. Crown would come home from work, go hunting, and come back with four or five squirrels. I remember him putting newspaper on the garage floor. He then would skin and gut the squirrels, and Mrs. Crown would cook them in a mixture of vegetables and voila! They had squirrel soup for dinner.

We even stayed on the Crowns' property in our camper while our new house was being finished. One day after school, Jeff shot an arrow from his dad's bow straight up in the air. Just like the old saying, what goes up must come down. It came down and stuck in the roof of our camper! I thought for sure Mr. Crown would hit him, beat him with a belt or something, like my dad would have done, but he didn't. He examined the small hole that had been made, put a tire patch on it, and took the bow from Jeff. He did threaten to come after him with his belt, but that never came to be. At dinner, they talked about how dangerous that was. His punishment was that he could not go catch nightcrawlers for two weeks. All of us kids loved helping Mr. Crown catch nightcrawlers that he would then sell for a little extra money. He'd also keep some aside for our frequent fishing trips. I really loved being a part of this family's activities. It was a way to escape the turmoil in my house and experience things that my father would never consider doing. We would also watch TV shows at their house in the afternoons. I saw every episode of *The Andy Griffith Show* and *Mayberry RFD*. The small-town atmosphere and feel-good story lines made me ache inside for a more stable home life. I couldn't help feeling a bit sad watching little Opie go fishing with his father at the beginning of each show.

Things changed a little in the next house we moved to. Mom still slept on the couch to thwart nighttime visits from my father and he still slept in the basement, but in our new house, the basement was finished, complete with a sliding glass door that led to the in-ground pool. Mom began to develop her own routine, which seemed to make her happy. If Dad came home drunk, she would pack up my sister and me in the Pontiac and drive around the mountain until daylight. I guess it was her way of avoiding fights and keeping us from watching Dad's self-destructive behavior. It was an interesting tactic and one that us kids didn't really mind. It felt like a new adventure every time and I loved driving by other small mountain homes, imagining what life was like with the families tucked inside, lights twinkling in the clear night sky. Mom also started a new shift that kept her away during the day, so with very little contact between the two, the fighting between my parents slowed considerably.

Since we had moved, we now had a new babysitter who would take me skiing at Greek Peak Mountain Resort almost every weekend. We also went to spring nationals in Indianapolis for National Hot Rod Association (NHRA) drag races. All of these activities made me feel much more like a regular kid getting to experience the things I had always dreamed of doing with my dad. He did take me and Sis to some stock car races, mainly because that was something he enjoyed, but he would always drink too much so we'd ride home smelling the rancid odor of motor oil and stale beer.

Sometimes we would stop by the Apalachin Hotel on the way home. Sis and I would remain huddled under a blanket in the backseat of the brown Ford Pinto station wagon to keep warm as Dad sat at the bar downing more beer. There was an old cowboy named Tex who would walk around the building drinking whatever was left in the open bottles strewn around the parking lot. One night, Sis and I were sleeping in the backseat when we heard a lot of noise and felt the car shaking. We peeked out from the blanket to see that a fight had broken out and one man was slamming the other into the battered Ford Pinto. We saw a man on his hands and knees look up with his bloody face only to receive a kick square in the chin and out he went. I thought for sure he was dead. We were terrified and pulled the blanket back over us, afraid for our lives. Fortunately, Dad ran outside and took us to the safety of our new home, then he climbed back in the car and returned to the hotel.

Our violent home life definitely affected me at an early age. There were times when I was mean to my sister for no reason. It's something I regret now, but it was the only behavior I saw so it started to feel normal, like everyone behaved that way. One time my mom lit her Viceroy 100 with a match and went out to hang clothes. My sister was maybe one and a half or two years old. I made my way over to her crib where she stood with her little fingers curled over the top rail. I held a lit match to her fingertips. She immediately started wailing louder than I'd ever heard from her. I ran over to the couch and pretended to watch TV. Mom came running up the stairs and instantly looked at me and said, "What did you do to her?"

I responded, "Nothing, honest, she always just cries for no reason I guess." Mom didn't ever tell Dad—at least I don't think so. Another time my sister was home for two months straight because she was diagnosed with a bone disease called osteomyelitis. This is a disease that eats away at the bone. Sis had collapsed in school one day and was confined to a wheelchair for a while. The kids at school all sent her get-well cards and the school sent her homework. I figured I could spice up her life a little while Mom and Dad were away. I was probably eight or nine at the time and I wheeled my sister over to the stairs that led down to Dad's dungeon. I proceeded to taunt her by pushing the chair to the first step and yelling, "I'm going to push you down the stairs! Watch out now, it's a long way down there. Are you ready?" She was terrified, and rightly so. She was crying pretty hard. I realized how helpless she was and how terrified she was. I quickly apologized and tried to be as nice as I could so she wouldn't tell on me.

By the time I was twelve, I was regularly driving my dad when he really got drunk, which was often. I remember his friends walking him to the car and sitting him in the passenger seat. "Let the kid drive. At least he'll get home in one piece," one of his drinking buddies would say.

Oddly enough, Dad began to take us on skiing trips. One weekend it was just him and me. Dad never really went skiing. He just loaded up the skis and wore a nice ski sweater, never even bothering to buy a lift ticket. The bar at the resort opened at noon and he became a regular there. I remember driving him home one night and I got lost, but there was a good reason for that. I had started drinking a little myself. Just like I saw Tex do at the hotel bar, I'd find bottles that still had some beer in them and quickly chug them down before any adults saw me. Or if they did see, they didn't care. That night I was buzzed and didn't have a clue where we were, so I pulled into the center of the highway where the cops would park. With the buzz I had, I ended up falling asleep. I was awakened by my father yelling. He was madder than a wet hornet. "Where the hell are we? Ah, for Christ sake, Kraig, can't you do anything right?" Luckily, in those days there weren't a ton of cops around.

The only time Mom and Dad acted cordial toward each other was around the holidays. We would go to see my mom's parents, Signe and Uno Bengds in Pleasant Mount, Pennsylvania. They had a two-hundred-acre farm with the old-style fieldstone fences that separated the fields. Dad was the only one who smoked in my grandmother's house. My mom smoked, but never during our holiday visits. My mom's sister and brother would be there with their families. I remember playing house with my cousins Sue, Marie, and Ellen. Somehow, we were on the swing set and I slapped Sue in the face for discipline, which of course at our house was quite normal. Uncle Buddy came out on the porch and waved me over to him. He crouched down and said in a strong whisper, "If I ever see you hit one of my girls again, I'm going to tan your hide but good!" I looked up at him with frightened eyes as he said, "Do you understand?" I nodded. "Okay," he added, "Go on and play now. Dinner will be ready soon."

Going to my mom's parents' farm was such a wonderful experience each and every time I went, even if I did occasionally get into trouble. My grandparents both came to America from northern Finland. They mostly spoke Swedish due to some kind of migration from Sweden to Finland during one of the early wars. In Finland, they lived in a small town called Narpes. All the residences spoke both Swedish and Finish. Grandma and Grandpa Bengd came over on separate boats and met for the first time on Ellis Island. Given how small Narpes was, they couldn't believe they did not know each other in Finland. Eventually, my grandfather helped build the original subways in New York City. My grandma took care of wealthy families by cleaning, cooking, and helping with their children.

Sheepshead Bay in Brooklyn, New York, was my mom's hometown, and when Grandma and Grandpa decided to buy a farm in northern Pennsylvania, my mom was devastated. She was seventeen and very adjusted to city life. Her pet peeve at her new, rural Preston High School was the cows. She hated milking the smelly beasts, but dutifully worked side by side with her younger sister, her brother, and her parents as they built their dairy farm into a nice little business with over two hundred head of Holsteins, two barns, several pigs and chickens, and a huge garden. The farmhouse was absolutely beautiful. The living room could be partitioned off from the dining room and the piano room with solid oak sliding doors that disappeared into the walls. The kitchen had a pass-through window so you could easily get food and dishes to and from the kitchen. There was also a dumbwaiter for hoisting prepared foods to the upstairs. The dining room was anchored by a beautiful hand-crafted table and chairs that sat twelve and more when scooted close together. The house also had a laid stone foundation and a huge stand-up attic where a kid could get lost for hours reminiscing among the antique crank phones, old 1920s clothes, trunks loaded with old toys and other treasures that time had surpassed, and Grandma and Grandpa didn't want to part with. Each of the upstairs bedrooms was furnished with huge beds framed by hand-carved posts on the corners. They also had a dresser and vanity with a three-mirror foldout for my mom and aunt. My uncle's room was outfitted for the boys with some toys scattered in the closet and an old chemistry set for experimenting.

We spent a lot of summer vacations on that farm. I sometimes took a friend of mine along with us for the adventure. Jeff came one summer. Ron another and PJ, who was my new friend when we moved into our new house. They all went home with great stories of working on the farm, swimming at a small lake nearby, and fishing in some awesome swampy ponds where the largemouth bass would bend our poles over like we were deep-sea fishing!

Grandpa took me everywhere on his John Deere tractor. I always thought of him as the strongest man in the world when I watched him start the tractor with his hands. He would flip a lever on the motor, spit on his palms, and roll the metal starting wheel back a little till it made an *ohowish-ohowish* sound. (I later found out this was opening the compression release and getting the motor on the compression stroke.) Then he would pull on the metal wheel with all his might and most of the time it would pop right off. If it didn't, he would mutter, "Oh ya ha," and get it on the next try. We also lived near a farm on Long Creek Road, and I often took the knowledge I got from Grandpa back to our home and picked up some part-time work on the Ames' farm in Apalachin.

These were wonderful times for me and a welcome escape from the turmoil at our house. Grandpa also taught me to cut hay and fix stone fence. I liked fixing the fences because I could move stone and stack pretty good. Grandpa also split wood by hand and sharpened knives on the pedal-driven grinding stone in the basement. Occasionally, some of his Swedish friends would stop by to shoot the breeze. For his entire life, he never got the hang of using the telephone. My grandma always dialed the phone for him.

Grandma worked in the fields turning windrows of hay over with wooded teeth rakes. When I wasn't helping Grandpa, I'd work by her side and cherish those long talks we had under the punishing sun. Grandma never talked to me about Mom and Dad fighting. I'm sure she was aware and knew it was a strain on us kids, and in return just offered her love. I think that's one of the reasons they tried to get us to the farm as often as possible. It was their way of offering a safe haven, if only temporarily.

Grandma taught me Swedish and always told me I would grow up to be a fine man. I loved her and Grandpa so much. I often wished I could just stay there. I sometimes would try to take a break and go to the farmhouse to get a drink. My grandma would stop me and show me how sucking on hard candy would quench my thirst. She kept several pieces of the treat in the pockets of her long farm dress for just such an occasion. The hay we had to turn was the leftovers that Grandpa couldn't get to with the tractor.

Grandma milked most all the cows on her own as the head count of their Holsteins fluctuated between seventy-five to two hundred based on the seasons and market prices. Grandpa handled the feeding chores and hay bale tossing. He also carried the Surge stainless steel tanks full of cow milk to the milk house and poured them through a paper strainer into the metal milk cans with "BENGDS" stamped in the lids. This was the only sanitary precaution in the 1960s. The milk was poured through the paper strainers and that kept flies and other bugs from getting into the milk cans. Grandma had one of those three-legged milking stools that Grandpa had made from a slab of wood. She moved from cow to cow with speed and precision, a stainless-steel bucket in one hand, a rag in the other, and a handful of cats following her every move.

She would use the rag to clean the cow's udders before inserting them into the suction tubes that coaxed the milk from the cows and emptied into the hanging tank. The cats would follow her, hoping for one of the rare occasions when she would aim a full udder at the loitering felines on the other side of the shit trough. They would eagerly open their mouths in anticipation of the random stream of milk. Grandma would start at one end of the cat line and expertly hit the eager mouth of each one, like one of those carnival games where you shoot water in the clown's mouth to blow up a balloon.

She acted like they were a nuisance, but Grandma loved those cats. She would fill a ham tin in the morning and at night, and leave it out as a treat. Any time there was a litter of kittens, she would make sure to leave out more tins to accommodate the growing herd. Once when it reached three tins, Grandpa put his foot down. He didn't care for the cats, but he realized their usefulness in keeping the mouse and rat population down around the barns. As was the practice on most farms back then, he had a crude way of dealing with the ever-growing pet population. During our chores, we would be instructed to grab a burlap sack from alongside the feed box. We had to collect seven to ten kittens from here or there, toss a field stone in the bag with them, and drop the sack in the water trough. I would stay behind, watching the sad bubbles pop on the surface, fast at first and then slowing after a couple of minutes. Grandpa would call, "Come on, Kraig, we have work to do."

As we got older, we could go to the farm over the Christmas vacation. Grandpa and I would visit the neighbors on the John Deere. I'd hold a Swedish coffee cake that Grandma had made with one hand, the other wrapped around the base of the seat to keep from falling off. During those visits, we got to see everyone's Christmas trees and presents. It was exciting to watch all of the families full of joy and holiday anticipation. Grandpa would pull us all to the top of one of the big hills on the back of the farm. Then we would zoom down on sleighs at fantastic speeds. I remember being so happy when Grandma knitted the kids wool mittens and scarves for Christmas. Then we could go sledding even longer! If we got tired, we would take a break at the farmhouse with a plate full of cookies and mugs of piping hot chocolate. Then for the last bit of fun, we would go to the lower flat field where Grandpa had driven an eight-inch section of tree into the ground. He slid a pipe over the post and somehow attached a twenty-foot, eight-inch log horizontally. On the outer end was a box that would hold two or three kids in it. Once situated in the box, he pulled the John Deere's nose between the box and the pole and started pushing on the log. Round and round we would go until it was time to change riders or get gas for the tractor.

Since Grandpa was such a good carpenter and craftsman, he had made us a huge teeter-totter that sat two on each end. I remember riding on the teeter-totter with two of my cousins and my sister. Sis was on the backseat behind me and my cousins on the other end. With one leap, I jumped off as we hit the ground. When I jumped off, our end went up in the air super-fast and my sister was hurled in the air like a flying squirrel. She landed with a hard thud about halfway to the other side and started crying real loud. I tried to say I fell off, but my cousins knew better so I had to admit to the dirty deed. I got plenty of finger flicking from Dad after he heard about it, not to mention a few harder hits from his hand on the back of my head on the way home. I did feel bad that my sister got scraped up pretty bad.

No matter how wonderful and exciting our farm visits were, that elated feeling quickly melted away as we sat glumly in the backseat while Dad drove us home. We knew it was only a matter of time before we would be back in that house full of violence and rage. My only salvation was counting the days until I would be able to go back to my grandparents' farm. Once, after we returned home, my mom was somehow draped over the edge of the bathtub and Dad started slamming the shower door back and forth into her rib cage as she screamed in pain. I was actually relieved when they divorced in 1976. Dad had arranged to have the divorce papers served to Mom at work. As she pulled into the driveway that day, my father flipped her the bird while taking a sip from his Budweiser. In a fit of rage, she swerved the car toward him, causing him to jump behind a large stone that fortunately stopped the Toyota from pinning him against the house.

It took fifteen years after that for them to get along well enough to talk and be civil. I went to live with Dad and Sis went with Mom. I grew my hair long after graduating from high school, which was the style back then. Dad came home drunk and apparently his friends at the bar had been poking fun at him for having a hippie son living with him. He barged into my room, grabbed my hair, and dragged me out of bed. "Get this mop cut," he yelled. I was so upset and so tired of his abuse that for the first time, I retaliated. I punched him with all my might right in the nose and broke it. Blood shot out the side of his face. He was stunned at first, but that didn't stop him. As he grabbed a cloth to control the bleeding, he continued to hurl insults at me. I moved out the next day.

I was tired of the way he had treated me, but I did want to continue our relationship as adults. He was my father after all. I still called him and went to his house for holidays, but it felt good to be out on my own. We continued our relationship with varying degrees of contact until his death on October 19, 1999, when he succumbed to cancer. I had sat at the edge of his bed for weeks letting him know how good of a father he was and how I would always remember the camping trips, ski trips, and stock car races he took me to. He reached out, grabbed my hand, and thanked me for saying that. He told me he knew my sister and I had a tough life as kids. He understood it was "a living hell" as he put it, and he was right about that. My sister came to visit him as well and he told us both that he really did love us, something he rarely if ever said when we were kids. We all hugged, realizing that this would likely be our last embrace.

It felt like everybody had a "normal" family except for us. To this day, my aunts and uncles and their children all seem to have very typical families with regular lives. My cousin Kendra went on to marry Franklin Graham's son, Will. My mom called me when I was living in California. She said we had a wedding to go to. I suggested I send my son, Rob, on a plane to Tucson where the wedding was, and Mom could pick him up. She said, "You listen to me, mister, my brother's daughter, your cousin Kendra, is getting married to Billy Graham's grandson. That's Franklin's son. They'll both be at this wedding and you will be too because it's as close to God as you'll ever get!"

Rob and I both went to the wedding.

4

THE TRUMP TRAIN

The Trump Train in Iowa was hard work. I flew out on January 6, 2016. I remember it well because it was two years to the day from when I had lost Rob. A rally in Urbandale was on the calendar for us to visit. The rally was held at Living History Farms Visitor Center with room for about 2,500 to 3,000 supporters. It was at this rally that Mr. Trump promised me, in honor of my son, that he was going to fight the opioid crisis. He was also going to make healthcare more affordable with lower deductibles, reduced overall cost, and better coverage.

When we were in Iowa, we had to protect the sides of the truck from possible vandals. Those events were unpredictable to say the least, so we tried to make sure we were prepared for anything that might happen. One distraught anti-Trump protester could ruin the image that wrapped around the truck with a can of spray paint or a sharp object scraping down the side. For protection of the truck at night, the artist bought a huge blue tarp, some nylon rope, and fifty or so bungee cords. We fastened a thirty-five-foot length of rope to the eyelets of one side of the tarp—one on each end and three in the middle, spaced apart—five lengths of rope in all. Every night we would pull the frozen tarp from the back of the truck where it sometimes became buried under the prints, bumper stickers, and other items that were used during the day at a rally or town-square event that was held in small towns across Iowa. The tarp was unfolded on one side of the truck and we tossed the rope lengths over the top. We then would go to the other side and pull on the ropes, dragging the tarp over and down the other side of the truck. The ropes were tied fast to the frame and the bungee cords were used to draw tight every loose part of the tarp so that the swift winds could not peel it away. That would make it difficult for would-be vandals to gain access to the precious image. Every morning we would have to reverse this process before we hit the road for more Trump-inspired activities.

Being a trucker myself, I understood the value of a vast network of fellow travelers, so I talked to the artist about getting a CB radio to communicate with the many semi-drivers that we had seen during our travels. He finally agreed and once it was installed we created an online meet-up event aimed at our new friends called "A Convoy for Trump." We were hoping to help build followers and spread the word about Trump so that when he held another rally, there would be even more attendees. Since it was his truck, the artist made most of the plans and he mapped out a route that would take us through Des Moines. I understood the challenges of driving a big truck, and I knew the small streets and tight curves were not trucker-friendly. I tried to offer my opinion as to the best routes for our new friends, which was to avoid city driving at all costs, but the artist knew best. Unfortunately, when the truckers found out where we wanted them to go, most of them backed out. The event was not much of a success and the few truckers who did make it only stayed briefly and then headed back to the highway to continue their journey. Our first attempt at drumming up support was a bust.

One interesting thing that happened was a Japanese film crew showed up and asked if they could join us on our travels. We found out that news about the rallies had traveled all over the world, and foreign journalists were eager to learn more about this unconventional political approach. Someone from the Associated Press also showed up and asked me if I was the guy who had lost my son to heroin. Apparently, my interaction with Trump had made its way into many news stories and headlines. When they found out I was in fact that guy, they asked me to stand in front of the graphics on the truck and play some songs about Rob as well as a few Trump songs that I had written for the rallies. I was then interviewed by a half-dozen journalists from local and world news outlets. It was quite a whirlwind of activity and something that caught me completely off guard. I knew that the media was interested in this undeniable groundswell of support for Trump, but with all of the polls saying that he would never be a candidate, much less the president, I never expected so much attention.

After it was all over, the artist sat me down and explained he did not appreciate me using his Trump truck as a backdrop for my photos and interviews. This was the first time I felt friction between the two of us. I thought we were getting along well and working toward the same goal, but apparently, he was having a problem sharing the attention. The only coverage he got from that day was an article in *GQ Magazine* and it wasn't particularly flattering. The headline read "Meet Trump's Ragtag Army of True Believers in Iowa," and it did have a picture of his painting on the side of the Trump truck, but once again they had me playing my guitar and singing in front of it, so he wasn't even featured. The article basically scolded us for advertising a huge event where no one showed up.

Undeterred, we continued on our venture and our next stop was Walker, Iowa. There, we ran into the General, a veteran and farmer in his eighties who had lost his wife and was looking for something to occupy his time. We had met him at the Trump painting unveiling in Des Moines at the recreation center rented by the artist for the event. The General wore his uniform proudly and was a diehard Trump supporter. He offered his farm to us as a place to rest and regroup. We took him up on the offer and enjoyed listening to his stories.

As I talked with the General, I realized that those of us declaring our support for Trump—this brash, untested, traditionally unpresidential candidate—had some commonalities. All of us had experienced a recent loss or tragedy and were looking for a way to channel our frustrations. We needed to fill a void in our lives, whether we realized it or not, and for some reason, the unrehearsed, often ill-planned, and frankly amateur way that Donald Trump and his team approached the election process appealed to us. We saw in him someone who was out of his element, who was not the typical, polished, TV-ready politician which we were all familiar with. Granted, he was wealthier than any of us would ever be, but we still connected with him and felt like he understood us and our plight. He was obviously the odd man out in the overcrowded pool of Republican candidates jockeying for the party nomination, and that was appealing. He hadn't delivered the carefully crafted answers that most candidates rattled off without even trying. He seemed to be speaking from his heart. I didn't always agree with what he said or how he said it, but

I damn sure respected the hell out of his willingness to do it his own way, probably much to the chagrin of his campaign managers.

The General told us about a small town that was close to Walker and had a population of about eight hundred. I remember him saying as we were driving, "This is Ryan, Iowa. They don't even have a grain elevator. You ain't nothing if you don't have a grain elevator!" The three of us went to a Trump rally in Cedar Falls and it was a frigid three degrees that morning. The rally wasn't scheduled to start until 6:00 p.m., but we had set out early to start some stumping for Trump along the way. The General was in uniform and was so happy that in a few hours he would be able to see his candidate. We ate breakfast prepared by our host that morning and set out. We stopped at a couple of mom-and-pop grocery stores along the way, chatting about Trump and connecting with the locals. We arrived at the University of Northern Iowa at noon. The temperature had crept up to the low teens by then. There were not a lot of supporters in line, and I'm sure the temperature wasn't helping to bring people out. Nonetheless, security was in place and we were waved to the front of the main entry for the rally. Apparently, maybe because of the General's uniform and our official-looking truck, we were mistaken for part of the actual campaign.

That made sense because everywhere we went, people would immediately surround the truck and start taking pictures, and that included the media as well. When the people in those small, Midwest towns and cities looked and saw the words printed alongside the painting, "God has chosen Donald J. Trump to be our next president," they often gave pause. While they were eager to support Trump for president, many of them reminded us that there was only one God.

In Cedar Falls, before the rally, I grabbed my guitar and went to play music for the line of shivering supporters as it wended along the wall of the building. Then I jumped back into the heated cab of the truck, joining the artist and the General to get warm before going back out. Two hours before the doors were to open for the rally, the General and I secured our place in line and then I began playing guitar while the General watched, smiling, as he saved my place in line.

Once inside, we went to the front of the stage and waited for another two hours. By the time the rally was supposed to start, there was not a whole lot of people inside. It seemed the fire marshall had been turning a lot of folks away for some reason. Clearly there was a mix-up since the facility could easily hold many more than were let in. Trump later explained from the stage that this was an example of "rigging," a subject he would frequently harp on during his time in front of the audience. I noticed that what sounded like complaining was something he did at almost every single rally. There were complaints about the way he (and by association his supporters) was treated by "the media," which seemed to be a catchall for anyone or any organization that did not support his agenda.

That was when I began to wonder if I had made the right choice in supporting this man. I wasn't prepared to give up on him because, after all, he had promised in front of everyone that he would help with the heroin and opioid epidemic, and that was my true passion. However, I didn't like the negativity and name-calling. By going to every single rally, I heard all of them often, and much of it was repetitive. At every rally I attended, he referenced the media as being "scum of the earth" and "they should be ashamed of themselves," sometimes adding things like "well, maybe not you, Jim" or "some may be bigger scums than others." He was always pitting the supporters against the media and prompting them to boo and curse the dedicated media crews who showed up at every rally and set up behind the supporters on the ground floor on an elevated platform.

It gave me an uncomfortable feeling because I had begun to have more and more interactions with the media, and I was usually treated well. The stories may not have been exactly as I would have reported them, but I respected the work. Trump didn't feel that way. He cursed the media and at the same time used them to give him an upper hand against his opponents as they offered free TV coverage every time he uttered an insult or ridiculed an adversary. It seemed that as soon as he realized how the game was played, he ratcheted up the insults. He would propose outrageous, crazy agendas if he were to be elected president, and that just increased his exposure by those very organizations that he was targeting in his speeches. It was surreal to watch from the ground level. I could see that Donald Trump was developing a keen affinity for how and when to get more free exposure. It was a smart business move because his campaign didn't have to resort to the multimillion-dollar advertising that his opponents used.

After a few guest speakers took the stage, Donald Trump made his grand entrance with "Eye of the Tiger" playing loudly over the speakers. He strutted down the walkway that led to the main stage with spotlights following his every move and Secret Service agents all over the place. It was a nightmare for them from the beginning because the rule of no red focus lights from cameras had not been put in place yet (or people just didn't obey the rule) because Donald Trump had red dots now and again glowing on his body from these beams of light. The problem of course was that they looked like the red beams from a rifle scope. Everyone up front had their cameras and phones focused on Mr. Trump. He obviously enjoyed every minute of the attention. A celebrity in every sense of the word, he fit the mold of every politician that ever ran for office, despite his claims to the contrary.

We were exhausted but energized the day after the rally. The General and I were on the front page of *The Drudge Report* news site. I had made sure that the General got Mr. Trump's autograph, which pleased him to no end. I got one for myself on my CD of Christian music. After we celebrated the article, the artist and I dropped the General off at his house and continued our journey. The artist plotted out a course that would take us to the four corners of Iowa and every place in between. Despite my growing reservations, I was excited about the whole thing and couldn't wait to get out and talk about Mr. Trump and how he was going to "Make America Great Again." I had bought into the entire philosophy right down to the ambiguous but noble-sounding tagline.

On January 19, 2016, Ames, Iowa, was the location of the next rally. It was at the Hansen Agriculture Executive Learning Center. One of the special guests was Sarah Palin, who had recently announced her endorsement of Donald Trump. The rally was scheduled for a 6:00 p.m. start time with the doors opening at 4:00. We arrived in Ames a day early after spending most of our time on the phone trying to secure a home where we could spend the night. The artist had called a friend in Florida and sold him one of his prints and a campaign poster that I had gotten signed at the Cedar Falls event. With that windfall, we stayed at a Holiday Inn. By 7:00 that evening, it was a bone-chilling five degrees and the wind was gusting at fifty mph. As we tossed the ropes over the truck, the wind picked up the blue tarp and tossed it to the far end of the parking lot. We ran after it, slipping and sliding on the ice and snow along the way. Fortunately, it got hung up on a light pole at the edge of the parking lot. I suggested we just stow the tarp back in the truck as the chances of vandals being out that night were slim, but the artist insisted we get it secured. My hands and toes were frozen by the time we finally tightened the tarp. Since I had never planned to stay in Iowa this long, all I had for warmth were my Justin Full Quill Ostrich cowboy boots and a thin leather jacket. I had bought a pair of gardening gloves at a local convenience store to keep my fingers from freezing off, but I was not prepared for this type of work.

The next day, we were excited for another rally. We checked out of the Holiday Inn and found a nice little cafe to eat breakfast. The artist went from table to table and asked them what they thought of Donald Trump. It seemed that, initially, most of them either didn't care for Trump or didn't want to be bothered, but after talking with the artist some would come around and by the end of the conversation they were asking for a bumper sticker or postcard.

At the Ames rally, things started out the same. We were allowed to park right up front again, where all the people were waiting. After playing guitar for the people in line and telling my story about losing Rob to heroin, I went back to the truck to get warm. The artist said it was time for me to get in line and go inside. By this point, he had decided that getting rid of me would allow him to get some interviews. He was surprised when I told him I was having a great time and elected to stay and continue to play for the supporters in line. I was getting so much satisfaction from being able to talk about my son and tell folks about how good of a man he was before I lost him to heroin. It felt reassuring to have people express their support and condolences. I was able to spread the word about Rob and that helped to keep his spirit alive, and that was the most important thing I could do. As cold as it was, the supporters loved the music and even sang along. It seemed to take their minds off the cold temperatures. As usual, there were opportunistic vendors selling Trump-themed wool hats, scarves, gloves, sweat suits, jackets, even Trump socks. Everyone was eager to make some money off the name Trump or the ever-present slogan, "Make America Great Again."

The rally started with about three thousand people still out in the cold. Donald Trump's team instructed security to sweep another auditorium for bombs before funneling the remaining supporters into the alternate rally area. There were big screen TVs for everyone to watch and see what was happening in the main rally. When Donald Trump finished with his speech, he walked next door and did the whole thing over for those folks who weathered the cold to see him. We could hear the cheers from inside the cab of the truck. This was something everyone was talking about, and if you were on the fence about your support for Trump when you came to this rally, you were on the Trump Train by the time you left. It was simply amazing to watch the vibrant mood swing when he did give his performance for the good folks of Ames, Iowa.

As I witnessed this almost religious experience that people had in response to the Trump message, it helped to reassure me that I was doing the right thing by supporting his campaign. This man was going to fulfill his promise to me and that was my main objective. Keeping Rob's name alive by performing was amazing, but having someone who could potentially become the president of the United States promise to help was something I couldn't ignore.

Next, we traveled around Iowa visiting local town squares in any small town we could find. We also went to gun shows, car shows in malls, grocery stores, diners—anywhere we thought there might be like-minded people who wanted to talk about the Trump windstorm blowing through the Midwest. It was difficult finding places to stay, but we continued relying on the kindness of strangers to put us up for a night or two.

In Ottumwa, a nice couple allowed us to stay on their farm. Larry had attended the unveiling of the painting in Des Moines and offered his farm to us whenever we were in town. The artist had not planned a lengthy stay in Ottumwa, but since we had accommodations, we went with it. Larry took us to his preacher's house in the morning.

He said, "Listen to this man [the artist]. He says Trump is chosen by God. I believe him because it's in the Bible. You see, Isaiah 45 says some things that resemble what's going on with Trump. In Isaiah 45, God says to Cyrus, 'Cyrus, I anoint you to overcome kingdoms. Even though you do not know me, I anoint you to rule and no one shall stop you.' It's something like that without looking it up," he said, lowering his head and waiting for a response. The preacher was not in agreement with this analogy. He told Larry that he thought Trump was a fraud and was not going to vote for him. Dejected in front of us, his new friends, Larry thanked the preacher for his time. He then took us to meet a few more of his friends, ones who were more or less

38

in agreement with his line of thinking. Then we returned to the farm where his gracious wife, Char, had a wonderful home-cooked pot roast meal on the table. It was complete with homemade apple pie with a flaky crust that melted in my mouth.

These folks were truly wonderful to us, and I was disappointed by our abrupt departure. The next morning, after a good night's sleep in a comfy bed with several quilts piled on top, the artist indicated that he was ready to leave for the other side of the state. He then showed me a chipped part of the driveway and said he was worried that Larry would notice it soon. Apparently, he had pulled into the wrong end of the drive and as he made the corner turn, the truck's front tire went off the edge of the thin concrete, breaking a little piece. The artist never said anything about it so neither did I.

We got showered, dressed, and prepared ourselves for the drive to Sioux Center, Iowa, on the west side of the state. Char had fixed us eggs, sausage, and a plate of gravy and homemade biscuits with orange juice and coffee. I was ready to dig in, but the artist told Char and Larry that we didn't have time to eat. I sat down anyway and said grace with the couple while the artist went out to start the truck. I ate every bit of food put out for me and thanked them both for everything they had done for us. I was taken aback when the artist came back inside and said, "We have to leave now!" I was embarrassed in front of our hosts, but I hugged them both and followed my impatient driver to the truck.

Once I was in the cab, the artist made a phone call and we ended up sitting in the driveway for another fifteen minutes while he spoke with someone in Sioux Center. I later returned to Iowa, in the summer of 2016, and stayed for almost two weeks. That amazing and kind couple will be forever in my thoughts and prayers. I love them both and one day I might take them up on their offer to have me stay with them and help out on the farm. That would be such a peaceful lifestyle where all I'd have to do is help on the farm and play my Christian music at church every Sunday. While I was visiting for the second time, I did come clean and told them it was our truck that broke the driveway piece of concrete. We all laughed as we remembered how fast we had to leave on that cold January day.

The venue for the next rally, the one in Sioux Center, was the BJ Haan Auditorium at Dordt College, a private Christian school. We made it about halfway across the state and decided to pull over and sleep. Sleeping sitting up in the truck was not fun, but it was a necessity. We met up with a couple who invited us to their country home for dinner. She was a solid Trump supporter, but her husband couldn't stand him. He was very gracious to us, but it was clear that he was not overjoyed with these two Trump campaigners in his home. We were polite and ate quickly before heading out the door. The woman pulled us aside and gave the artist the phone number of her daughter and son-in-law who lived in a nearby town. "Call this number and ask for Janice. She's my daughter and I told her you were friends of mine and needed a place to sleep for the night."

I was continually amazed by the generosity of the people we met during our travels. We hardly knew this woman and she was sending us to stay with her daughter because her husband didn't want anything to do with us. Our only bond with these people was the belief that we were actually going to change the direction of this country. We had a hand in electing the next president of the United States. So, we called the number and got directions to their house. They were perfectly nice people and it was a brief stay. The next morning, we uncovered the truck and resumed our journey.

The next night, we again were looking for a place to sleep. It was difficult to cover a lot of territory because we were always taking the back roads and stopping when we saw a place where we could talk about the candidacy of Mr. Trump. When I think about our journey, it's rather amazing that we had somehow convinced ourselves to dedicate our time to promoting a politician's election to office for no compensation. We were giving ourselves to this cause that we were sure would benefit us in the long run. Finally, that night we were exhausted, but couldn't find a place to sleep. We didn't want to stay in the uncomfortable truck especially because it had started to snow, and we couldn't leave the engine running all night.

We were running low on money, so we did the only thing we could think of. We prayed. We stopped in the parking lot of Cronk's Diner in Denison, Iowa, and prayed. We prayed for guidance and help, and most importantly a place to lay our heads so that we could continue our important mission the next day. Once we were done, we drove around the corner and there was a motel. It wasn't the nicest place in the world, but I could tell someone had been trying to make improvements. The sign outside said weekly rates available. I went in and negotiated a Christian CD, a Trump art print, and $100 for us to stay there for as long as we needed to. I was so happy when the kind owner agreed to the deal. This unquestioned generosity continued to amaze me.

Having arranged such a sweet deal, we decided to stay at the motel until the caucuses. We were in Crawford County, right smack dab in the middle of Iowa. There were three meat-packing plants in the town of Denison that employed about one thousand illegals at $12 per hour. This was Cruz and Rubio country with very few Trump supporters. Fortunately for us, the motel owner was a supporter, which helped, but we soon discovered that none of the other people staying there spoke any English. They were workers at one of those meat plants.

However, we were fortunate that we had a place to stay and even two electric heaters, one for each of us, to stay warm in the drafty room. We also had to contend with a few roaches from time to time. Once, I was going to cook something in the microwave and roaches came from inside the side vents. It wasn't ideal, but it would do. We ended up staying for two weeks.

When we finally arrived at Dordt College, it was about 6:00 in the morning. We wanted to get there early for the 11:00 a.m. rally and be up front as we always did and promote Donald Trump to the supporters. It was a frosty two degrees that morning, and the artist had made arrangements for an interview with a Chinese TV station. They were going to ask him questions about the painting and what inspired him to paint it. He was very excited about the interview and the opportunity to promote his work. He instructed me to stay in the truck and out of the way. As we waited for this Chinese station, I played my guitar for the few scattered supporters that had begun to arrive. Then I went back to the truck. Normally under these circumstances, I would tell the guy to "take a long walk on a short dock," but I needed a ride home and I was dependent on him, so I did as he asked.

The crowd had swelled in size as it got closer to rally time and the media were everywhere. I was in the truck like a kid being punished. I started thinking, *What am I doing? Why am I forced to sit in here like a child? I have as much right to be involved as he does.* Finally, I had reached my breaking point, and as the artist's interview was underway, I jumped out of the truck and walked by the Chinese media. I also saw six or seven other journalists standing in front of the truck with microphones and cameras reporting on this Trump truck. As I walked by, the artist asked, "What do you think you're doing?"

I looked at him, his cameraman now holding his camera off his shoulder as if taking a break. "I'm going to the back of this truck, I'm getting my guitar, and I'm going to play songs for those thousands of people standing in line. That's the reason why I am here!"

With that I strapped on the guitar. I had on a shirt, my vest, jeans, and my Justins to keep me warm. I started wailing and singing one of the newest songs I had written. "Trump Train, keep a rollin', Trump Train, keep a rollin' on down the line." This was the first Trump Train song ever and they loved it. The crowd went wild. I would play for about one hundred supporters in line, and then move down to another group, trying to reach as many as possible. I didn't have an amp or microphone; it was just sweet. Even sweeter for me was to see all those reporters including the Chinese representatives come running to see what the fuss was all about. By that time, I was singing "Cherished Memories," which was a song I had written about Rob. Reporters lined up to get an interview with me. It was truly unexpected and overwhelming. I was just killing time while he finished his interview and now it was all about me. I did a live "Donald Trump for President" segment for Fox News. I also did interviews with many international reporters including those from Japan, German, Sweden, and even ones from China who had been over by the truck.

Between interviews, I looked over at the artist standing on the driver's side step that led to the cab of the truck. He was just gazing at the excitement I had created. It was clear to me after that day that I would need to figure out another way to continue this journey. I wasn't going to be staying in the truck anymore. While it sucked that it was basically a showdown between me and him, it was an unintended breakthrough for me. I was getting recognized for my contributions, not just for being in a boldly painted box truck riding across the country. I hadn't realized how important this attention was for him and his art. I thought it was all about the Trump candidacy, I thought it was about *the cause*.

I had planned to find a different ride, but the artist surprised me. He drove me back to Denison, and on the way, he talked about me joining forces with him. He even toyed with the idea of painting a picture of the two of us on the back of the truck. He didn't say a word about the shift of the reporters' focus. As we continued our discussion, I told him I was all for doing something together and we just needed to hash out the details. I was not currently paying any room or gas charges and I was sure this would change if I stayed on the truck indefinitely. I was fine with that as long as we discussed it in advance.

The next day, the artist's phone rang, and it was Trump Campaign Headquarters in Des Moines. They informed him that Eric Trump was coming to Iowa and wanted to visit Cronk's Diner. We had found out that Cronk's is a famous stopping place for politicians throughout history. Ted Cruz had stopped there, Marco Rubio, and hundreds of politicians before them. Eric Trump was coming to Cronk's, and they asked if the artist and I could accommodate him and his wife, Lara, during their visit.

Word had gotten around that we were able to generate support and garner media buzz in the name of Trump. We were given specific instructions. We were to meet his car in the parking lot and under no circumstances was he to walk unescorted to the front entrance. They also told us to open the door for Eric, Lara, and his handler or assistant.

By simply being validated by the campaign and recognized for our boots-on-the-ground mission felt very rewarding. Since we were acting on our own accord, we never knew if our actions were making a real impact on the campaign, until now. We advertised in the local paper and got the word out with posters and flyers. We even helped arrange for the local police department to be present to control protesters, if any. We worked together to pull off the best event possible. This was our chance to show the Trump organization what we could do. The event turned out better than expected, and I even got a picture of Eric and me together. I also played my songs before the event.

The artist set up his painting in the banquet room and Eric stood in front of it while he spoke and took questions from the audience of about seventy-five ardent supporters. It was very up close and personal with no real security other than the two cops we had recruited from Denison. There were some families who had relatives working at one of the meat plants that were afraid their loved ones would be deported and separated from their families. After they voiced their concerns, Eric promised this would not happen. He also told the artist he would see to it that his painting was displayed in the White House if his dad was elected. The artist was elated, and I couldn't blame him. This would be great exposure for him and his work. He was beaming with excitement and I couldn't believe how well the evening had turned out.

With the artist handling most of the organizing and me helping to sort out the details, we had worked together to create a very successful event, and the artist would gain some national exposure. It was amazing, and with renewed optimism, we eagerly went back to our homegrown campaign. We visited every Burger King and McDonald's we could find. There, we would always meet locals who were eager to listen to our message. They were also entertained by our new story of how we had just helped Donald Trump's son hold an event right here in Iowa. We even started going door to door like 1950s vacuum cleaner salesmen. It didn't matter to us. There were plenty of people willing to hear about Trump. Even those who weren't interested closed their doors with midwestern politeness. We stopped at barbershops, hair salons, gas stations, motorcycle shops, truck garages, basically anywhere that we found an audience. We even set up in front of grocery stores and in parking lots until a manager would come and ask us to leave. The thing that held me and the artist together was that common bond. We both wanted Trump to be the next president of the United States, and we would do whatever we had to in order to make it happen.

We then went to Des Moines for a debate scheduled for January 28, 2016. Trump was protesting Fox News because he felt they were pandering to his Republican opponents. He held a fundraiser for veterans at nearby Drake University. His whole plan was to impact the ratings of the scheduled debate for the other Republican presidential candidates jockeying for the party nomination. He apparently succeeded since the ratings were reportedly lower than expected. In fact, a few attendees of the GOP debate ended up visiting and speaking at Trump's veterans fundraiser event. Trump raised a ton of money for the vets, but had a hard time actually finding an organization that would accept the donation. It became clear to us that there was still much work to be done. Trump's verbal attacks and aggressive nature was turning some people off and tainting his campaign. They finally found an organization that agreed to accept the money, although it was almost seven months before the funds from the event were donated.

The artist and I went back to Denison and Crawford County. The caucuses were quickly approaching, and we needed to find caucus captains to help with the cause. The Trump campaign had no ground game in Iowa except for folks like us. We were the only ones with the time and determination to devote to the election. They had a headquarters where you could get signs and bumper stickers, but there wasn't a lot of community involvement. We went there one day to collect some promotional material and they only gave us ten signs. We were stunned. After all we had done, we could give those away in minutes. We needed more, lots more. Later, when they realized what we could do, they rewarded us with seventy-five of the precious signs.

It was finally time for the caucuses, and once it was over, Trump didn't win Iowa. It was a slight blow to our momentum, but we realized that Iowa was a proportional state. He got a good portion of the delegates, which meant there was still a long way to go. The count was Cruz leading with eight, and Trump and Rubio tied with seven each. Ben Carson had three and Rand Paul had one delegate vote. Since Cruz was the frontrunner, Trump lashed out that he was treated unfairly. He accused Cruz and his campaign of spreading rumors that Carson had dropped out, prompting Carson voters to caucus for Cruz.

I was learning a lot about our election process. Actually, this was the first election I had ever participated in, and it was a continuous learning experience. To me, the whole idea of the caucus is crazy. They split you up into groups and send you into a room to debate. It's like a jury in a court system. If there's one holdout, they try to convince you to change your mind. Carson and Trump did get cheated in more ways than one in Iowa. Each candidate was to have a certain amount of time represented by a spokesperson. This person would speak to the crowd, and when all the speakers were done, the people voted. Cruz had two reps talk to the crowd and both went over their allotted time. Cruz also had a professional speaker address the crowd as well. When we asked the foreperson, she said she had no idea this was going on and they would be more alert for the next election.

How did I know how this works? Simple, because I was there in the caucus rooms as it took place! The only thing I can say for sure is that we proved having a solid ground team worked since Crawford County, in the middle of Iowa, was Trump county when we were done with it. We really made a difference and our actions launched ground teams around the United States that were created by the Trump campaign, based on our success. Canvas crews would go up and down the streets, the whole nine yards. It became much more organized. It felt good that we had made a difference.

On the drive home to New York from Iowa, the artist and I talked about what was next. It was on our way back that the artist told me about the new deal he was proposing. I would have to pay him $3,000 per month to ride in the truck and go to the rallies. That would help cover his expenses. He also wanted me to sign a contract with him giving him 50 percent of any of my future Trump-based earnings. He wanted half of everything because he said I would never have been exposed to the Trump sensation without him. That's not necessarily true because I would have probably gotten involved in another way, but that wasn't the point. I asked him about the $3,000. I tried to be fair. I said, "I don't mind forking out $3,000 if you're going to pay me back half of everything I spend." That way we would truly be sharing the expenses, but he said no way.

I couldn't believe it. I didn't just say no, I said hell no. My daddy didn't raise no fool. Of course, I waited a day after I got home to tell him because I didn't want to get dropped off at some truck stop. I remember him coming to my house and asking me to sell my backhoe to help fund the journey. I just couldn't do it. I decided this was my time to regroup and come up with a game plan of my own.

I took some time to take in all that had happened over the last few weeks. I hadn't anticipated the attention and exposure to the media, and I wasn't seeking it like he seemed to be. My mission was deeper. I was searching for purpose. If all my life consisted of was waking up to go to work in order to pay an electric bill or something like that, it wouldn't be worth it. I wasn't ready to sell my construction equipment and other accumulated possessions. I needed something more, something deeper than any newspaper article or TV interview.

Now that I was back at home, I spent the first week of February playing undercover cop. I would park alongside a nondescript building or store and watch as drug deals went down right before my eyes. I saw a Chevy Blazer with Pennsylvania license plates pull up to a convenience store and then watched as a tall black male got out and engaged in conversation with a young white man that I knew Rob hung around with in his last days on earth. The two men talked for a short while and the black guy returned to the Blazer and drove off. I pulled out and followed him as he made his way down Spencer Avenue, which was notorious for drug activity. Rob's friend was already walking down the same street and I watched as the Blazer came to a stop. The guy on the sidewalk got into the Blazer and they continued down the road. They turned onto a little side street and the Blazer stopped again. Rob's friend got out and walked up to the door of a downstairs apartment. I wrote down the address and the license plate number of the Blazer as it sped off down the street.

I pulled over and called the Tioga County sheriff's office nonemergency line. I told the dispatcher what I saw, and she asked me, "What are you doing following people around?"

I told her, "I'm doing your job, lady. I'm watching for unusual activity in Owego." She supposedly took down the information from me and asked me to stop my amateur sleuthing and leave the police work to the professionals. Ten minutes later, I got a call from the sheriff's office and they asked me if I could meet with a deputy. I said of course I can and we met in the parking lot of a local pizza place. The deputy asked me about the Blazer again, and it turned out they had stopped him earlier that day for a minor traffic violation, failure to come to a complete stop at a stop sign. The deputy asked me to show him the exact door Rob's friend had visited. I rode with him and pointed out the apartment door. He showed me a picture of Rob's friend, who was a known dealer and had been under the sheriff's scrutiny for a while. He thanked me for the information and, like the dispatcher, asked me to not get involved as I might get hurt.

This incident helped me understand that whatever I did, it had to be for Rob and kids like him who have fallen prey to this evil world of drugs. That needed to be my focus, not just a presidential election. I felt good about what I had done and knew I had contributed to someone who had made me a promise to help with the country's drug dependency issues. I did understand that the police didn't want me interfering in their work. I decided that it was best if I return to the rally circuit, but this time on my own terms. However, I needed to come up with a way to finance myself. It was more important than ever for me to keep up the momentum from the previous rallies. There, I could talk about Rob, talk about the tragedies of drug addiction from a personal level, and also make a difference in Mr. Trump's campaign, which was really picking up steam at this point.

For guidance, I approached my friends at the cowboy church. I told them what I had learned and how I thought I could continue spreading the word about Rob and his tragedy. I suddenly felt good about everything when they told me if that's what was going to give me happiness, even if only temporarily, I should follow my heart. They refrained from telling me what to do, but offered their support to the idea if that's what I felt I needed to do to deal with Rob's death. That made sense to me and my mind was made up.

I was done thinking and ready to get started. I decided to sell my thirty-two-foot Jayco camper and construction job trailer loaded with tools. This would give me some seed money to get started. I struggled a little with the decision as I remembered the arguments I presented to the artist as to why I wouldn't do it for him. This was a big step for me. I had held off selling other items like my small dump truck and excavator thinking if things didn't work out I could regroup if need be and get back into the home foundation replacement business. I always wanted to have a fallback plan just in case I needed it. I put the camper and job trailer on craigslist and planned to monitor the response from the road. Then I was headed out on a 720-mile trip to Myrtle Beach, South Carolina. Donald J. Trump was scheduled to hold a rally at the Myrtle Beach Sports Center on February 19, 2016, and I was going to be there.

I set out for Myrtle Beach at 5:00 a.m. on February 18 and arrived at the Boardwalk Beach Hotel about 7:00 that evening. I made great time and was ready for the adventures ahead. The motel price was $69, which was the off-season rate for a room with no view. After I checked in, I drove a couple blocks to the Sports Center and checked it out. I had learned that it's best to get a lay of the land before things start to get hectic. Back at the hotel, I went to the restaurant next door and enjoyed a steak dinner and a vodka with cranberry juice. I had a second drink with my salad. The bill was $42 by the time I got done and with the tip it gobbled up one of the fifty dollar bills I had in my wallet. If I was going to do this, I was doing it right this time. I answered some calls about the camper and job trailer, telling them I would follow up when I got back to town. Trump had added Pawleys Island and North Charleston, South Carolina, to the next day's events. His campaign was heating up and I was determined to keep up as best I could. I quickly started calculating the distance to see if I could attend all three. Pawleys Island was only forty miles south of the Sports Center and from there it was another seventy miles to North Charleston. I was going to try to make all of them. I wouldn't be able to go inside the rallies, but I could play my songs, talk about Rob, and mingle with the supporters in line.

I got to the Sports Center at 7:00 the next morning. It was about forty degrees, which seemed like a heat wave compared to New York and a vast improvement over the cold in Iowa. There were only about five or six people in line for the noon event. I was surprised because the Iowa rallies seemed to fill up much faster, but I was interested in seeing what would happen. I played "Donald Trump for President" for the small audience and went right into my old country stuff—Hank Williams, Roger Miller, David Allan Coe, the classics. I continued to play and talked to the fast-growing line of supporters queueing up to hear their candidate speak.

As the crowd grew to about five hundred, by 8:30, one lady came up and hugged me after hearing the story of Rob and how he died from heroin. She laid her head against my shoulder and started crying gently as she told me through the tears she was sorry for my loss and thanked me for sharing. As she lifted her head up, she leaned in and whispered in my ear with an obvious attempt to keep what she was about to tell me between her and me.

She said to me, "We just lost our daughter Ellen to the same stuff." I had explained to the crowd that Rob died from a mix of heroin and fentanyl. Her Ellen had died from the exact same toxic mix. I pulled her close as tears started falling from my eyes now.

"I'm so sorry, ma'am. I wish there was something I could do to make the pain go away."

"Susan," she said. "My name is Susan, and this is my husband, Jack," as she wiped dry the tears from her cheeks. I did the same.

Jack stuck his hand out for a shake and said, "It's a commendable thing you're doing. I don't know how you can do it."

"It's not easy because I get emotional sometimes, but someone has to keep this topic in front of people or they will forget."

Jack agreed. "We're hoping Mr. Trump can do something about this stuff because it's everywhere."

Susan exclaimed, "Every other day it seems there is someone dying around here from drugs."

We nodded solemnly and talked some more before I moved on to another group of people. I still didn't have an amplifier or microphone, so my performances were raw and acoustic. The good thing was that, as I moved down the line to play for everyone, I was able to meet people individually. Those connections really helped to keep me going. Everyone was very supportive and encouraging. "That was a very emotional encounter, folks," I yelled to the final group. "How about a song called 'Donald Trump for President'?" I yelled. The crowd went crazy.

By 9:30, the crowd had grown to what seemed like thousands. I looked up and there were Trump campaign people handing out "Trump—Make America Great Again" signs to those standing in line. I glanced to the front of the line where I had started about two hours ago and couldn't believe my eyes. "General," I called out. "General, it's me, Kraig!" I rushed toward the short eighty-three-year-old, laid my guitar on the concrete sidewalk, and gave him a big hug, squeezing his handful of signs between us. I pulled back and said, "General, I never in a million years would have expected to see you here. How are you doing?"

He looked at me and smiled from cheek to cheek and said, "I filled out a form for the Trump campaign and offered to help if they could use me." He was so excited while telling me. "They called me a few days later and asked if I would travel with them to the rallies. I told them on two conditions," as he straightened up the signs he was holding. "I said all my expenses have to be paid for and I must be able to wear my uniform. So they flew me out here to South Carolina to work with the campaign!"

I could tell the General from Iowa had found something to occupy himself with and I knew that helped to take his mind off the recent passing of his wife. I thought that must be pretty hard to go through after being married for over sixty years to the same woman. Now it was just him in that huge, old farmhouse.

"Good for you," I said. "I'm so happy to see you again." As I turned to retrieve my guitar from the concrete sidewalk where I had laid it, a supporter had picked it up and was holding it like a dinner platter, waiting for me to take it.

"I hope you don't mind me touching your guitar, but it was getting scratched from being on the concrete."

I said, "No, not at all, and I thank you." The middle-aged man then asked me to play a tune. I had already played to this group, but I guess this guy had missed it so I dutifully banged out another "Donald Trump for President" since that was the most perfect song for the occasion. While I was singing, the General was handing out signs to the supporters.

After I finished he turned to me and said, "Where's the artist and his Trump truck?"

I said, "The artist had some other obligations and we kind of went our separate ways. I drove myself down here and I think I am going to cut out in just a little bit to go to Pawleys Island for the 3:00 rally. It was great seeing you and I wish you all the best."

The doors had opened at 10:00 a.m. and the crowd was moving steadily as it took some time to screen everyone going into the Sports Center. I played a little bit more and talked to a couple of local TV stations and let some journalists snap a couple pictures. "Well, I gotta go, folks," I yelled. "Headed down to Pawleys Island and play for those folks waiting to get into that rally." It wasn't as fun for me to play for people just walking by as they filed into the rally. I liked a captive audience, so I could tell Rob's story and mingle with the crowds that supported Mr. Trump. That was my mission and I planned to stick to it.

Off to Pawleys Plantation Golf and Country Club on beautiful Pawleys Island, South Carolina, which was about a forty-minute ride over about twenty-five miles. I got there at 11:15 a.m. for the 3:00 p.m. event. The crowd was not huge. There were about twenty-five or so people standing at the entrance of this old plantation mansion. The crowd was filing in steady and there was soon the typical circus-type atmosphere created by the many vendors that preyed on the supporters to buy Trump gear at a remarkably escalated price. I mean, people were buying red hats with "Make America Great Again" stenciled on the front for $15 each. These were $3 hats at best. Trump T-shirts started at $25 each and went as high as $40. These vendors were making a killing and most of them, as I later found out, didn't even like Trump. They were just there for the money.

As with many of these rallies, I noticed that there was not one black man or woman in line at the Pawleys Island Plantation House. With all the publicity of Trump being a racist, using this location for a rally was probably just too much for any supporters of color. They had a small area outside the property for the protesters. There were maybe fifteen or twenty holding signs that read "Trump's a Racist" and "Dump Trump." No one, including me, really paid any attention. I was met by a few journalists snapping my picture while I played my songs. A couple asked some questions about my cause and Rob's death. I didn't really mesh with the Pawleys Island folks. "A different clique of people," you might say. I did eventually get into playing for the supporters and some also shared their stories of knowing someone who had died from heroin, so it wasn't a lost cause, just a different vibe from the folks in Iowa.

Time had gone by pretty fast there, and before I knew it, Trump had arrived with his entourage. Black Cadillac SUVs pulled up to a cordoned-off side entrance. Mr. Trump got out of his vehicle as the crowd erupted in cheers. He turned to us and gave his signature one-handed wave with the other by his side. I thought about going into this rally at first, but then the doors closed and no one else was allowed in, leaving literally thousands of supporters disappointed. Large speakers were mounted on the outside of the white building, and after a while, the Rolling Stones, Elton John, Aerosmith, and other classic rock tunes started playing. It was just about 2:30 and the rally was scheduled to start at 3:00.

I headed to my truck, stopping occasionally to take pictures with the crowd as they asked for group photos with me. It was fun, but I had to hit the road since the next rally that day was seventy miles away.

I arrived in North Charleston, South Carolina, at 5:00 p.m. even though the seventy-mile trip was bumper to bumper at times. When I got to the North Charleston Convention Center, there was no one in line, not a soul. This place had a waiting area inside the building where people could be screened by the Secret Service. I just started playing outside the doors as stragglers entered the building. A Swedish TV crew asked me if they could do an interview about what I was doing. I was happy to talk to them and belted some Swedish I had learned from my grandma while working on the farm. "*Hur mår du*," I said, which means "how are you" in Swedish. We talked about my grandparents and where in Sweden they came from and then did the interview on-camera.

After we were finished, I went to the parking lot to check out this big eighteen-wheeler that read "TRUMP" on the side of its forty-eight-foot re-frigerated trailer with a beautiful Peterbilt truck hooked to it. I talked to the owner and asked him to snap a few pictures of me standing in front of it. I asked a campaign guy if I could have a few of the yard signs he was stabbing into the ground. He said I could take as many as I wanted from the ones he already put in the grass, but he couldn't give them to me directly. It was get-ting dark now, so I gathered about thirty yard signs to hand out back home some eight hundred miles away.

It was a long trip home and I drove straight through most of the night, stopping to sleep in the front seat of my Dodge pickup at a rest area at about

3:30 a.m. By 7:00 a.m., I was up and back at it. I arrived home at 5:00 p.m., very tired after chasing Trump all over South Carolina the day before. I was satisfied though. Had it not been for the Swedes (who were not allowed into the rally) and the Trump Truck, oh, and all the signs I got, North Charleston would have been a waste of time. Trump never allowed any foreign media into his rallies for some reason, which was just as well because that meant they would interview me. I was satisfied that I told Rob's story, and everyone listened and seemed to really hear my heart talking. I was glad to know I could do this on my own and I was just getting started.

I answered all the inquiries on the camper and job trailer that I had listed for sale and sold them quickly. That gave me about $5,000 in my pocket. I had a little time to get things together because the next rally I planned to attend was scheduled for February 29 in Radford, Virginia, at the Dedmon Center located on the Radford University campus. Columbus, Ohio, and Louisville, Kentucky, were also in my plans, but first I needed to talk to Roger and share my experiences in South Carolina.

People really received my message well. If they had not, I would have changed my plans because I only wanted to share with those interested in hearing. Heroin as it turned out was a much bigger problem in this country than I had originally thought. This was it, this was the purpose I was look-ing for. Donald J. Trump was my new hero and I would stop at nothing to convince everyone I met on the Trump Trail that Mr. Trump was the very best candidate for president. To make it more real and to keep me grounded on my mission, I kept Rob's ashes by my side while traveling since I would be doing this on my own. I had discovered that while I was helping Trump and his campaign, his rallies were helping me spread the word about this horrible addiction.

There were times when I wasn't sure I was doing the right thing, but as soon as I'd start playing and people would react so positively to my message, it helped reaffirm my direction in life. It felt like despite all that I had been through in my personal life, which culminated in the death of my only child, I was finally in a place where I could use my experiences to help others. Trump had promised that he would help me when he was elected, so it was only right that I help him when he needed it. Those rallies were cathartic for me as well. I felt like I could take on the world. I felt like Rob's death could make a difference in the lives of other people who still had a chance. I was channeling all of my painful memories into this mission, and I needed Trump and his rallies to provide purpose for my life. And more so, I hoped I could save a life or two along the way.

As I drove back and forth to those rallies with Rob's ashes by my side and his spirit in my heart, I couldn't help but think back to the past. I would think about the drama and craziness I went through, but I'd also think about that amazing day when I found out that I had a son.

5

CHERISHED
MEMORIES

In the late 1980s, I was driving a produce truck from California to different East Coast markets, mainly the Hunt's Point Market in the Bronx, New York City, and the Chelsea Market in Boston, which was when I met Rob's mom. Meeting her came at a time in my life when I was desperately in search of the family I had always hoped for growing up. I wanted a simple, drama-free home life totally unlike the dysfunctional one I grew up in. I wasn't asking for much, just a wife, kids, and two cats in the yard like the Crosby, Stills and Nash song "Our House" described back in the 1960s.

Suzi was a single mom with two kids of her own from a previous marriage when I met her. I was informally introduced to her by a fellow driver who was friends with her family and had a picture of Suzi, her mom, and the two boys—Jack and Derrick, ages seven and ten. He gave me the phone number of Suzi's mom and told me that Suzi was looking for the same thing I was, which was unconditional love. She was also hoping to find a stable home life for her children. When I contacted Suzi's mom, she told me I was a blessing because I first wanted to just help her out financially. My friend, who I only knew by his CB handle "Penny Pincher," had told me that Suzi was struggling to make ends meet as a single mom and could use help to get on her feet. As we talked on the phone, her mom told me that currently Suzi was in her car, which had broken down on Highway 20 just outside Big Springs, Texas, at a truck stop called Ripon Griffins. As a trucker, I knew this fuel stop very well and many of us referred to it as "Rip Off Griffins" due to their high prices on fuel and everything else. To their defense, truck stops popped up all over the place over the next five years, and by 1993, all the truck stops in the country had come to realize there was a lucrative market in supplying truckers with fuel and extra services.

I decided to meet Suzi and her two children on my way to Hunts Point. I was driving what they call a reefer trailer, which means it was refrigerated, since it was loaded with the finest California strawberries grown by the Driscoll Company. I also had six pallets of fresh raspberries in the middle of the trailer because they were most delicate, and we needed to keep them totally pristine for market. Riding in the middle of the load ensured the smoothest transport for the raspberries as there was very little road rumble in that location.

Having hauled produce for so long, I had become educated on the proper handling of this valuable cargo to ensure a successful cross-country delivery. Any kind of berry required delicate handling from cultivation to harvest to packaging, and especially as they are strategically loaded on the trucks in order to be promptly transported. They were loaded from a giant temperature-controlled building in the middle of the berry fields. My pickup location was around Watsonville, California, however, they had coolers in several locations outside of Santa Maria.

The workers were primarily from Mexico and some on work visas. These were the Mexican farmworkers everyone seemed to talk about and how they supposedly took jobs from Americans. I never agreed with Mr. Trump's plan for mandatory deportation of these immigrants since I knew they worked hard and performed the jobs that the farmers couldn't find others to do. I had seen it with my own eyes. These workers baked in one-hundred-plus-degree heat with pesticides and dust swirling around their sweaty bodies as they meticulously harvested each and every berry. Men and women both bent over in the fields with towels and T-shirts wrapped around their faces to filter the toxic air that surrounded them. These folks worked so hard just to live the American Dream. To me, that was inspirational.

When I finally pulled up to the truck stop, I saw a woman standing by a car and knew that must be her. Suzi was a beautiful, blonde California girl. She looked to be in her late twenties and was so pretty that I was immediately smitten. I introduced myself and began talking with her. She told me that she was sleeping in her Buick Regal, the car she was standing beside with a U-Haul trailer attached and that weighed the rear of the car almost to the ground. Her two kids, Jack and Derrick, were running around the parking lot playing some kind of tag and spraying each other with Silly String, that gooey mess that kids shot out of a can. I'm sure they were burning some pent-up energy. I tried to engage with them even though I didn't have a lot of experience with kids. Just as I turned to say something, wham! Jack, the youngest, stomped the toe of my snakeskin boots with his oversized Converse sneaker.

"Damn!" I yelled instinctively. "What the—why did you do that, you little peapod?"

They just thought that was the most hilarious thing, and both Jack and Derrick broke out in laughter. Then Jack asked, "Did that hurt?"

"No, it tickled," I said.

Suzi quickly scolded them and said, "Boys, that's enough!" Then she said to Derrick, "Get Mommy's cigarettes from the front seat of the car and get my soda while you're at it. Thank you, darling."

I asked Suzi where she was headed. She said that she was trying to get back to California, but her car had broken down. I started it up for her and there was a loud clanging noise from under the hood. I grabbed my tools, removed the valve cover, and found that one of the studs holding a rocker arm in place was broken, allowing the rod to bounce around unguided. I told Suzi she would need to go to a garage and I wanted to help her out. I gave her $300 to get her car fixed. "It shouldn't be much more than that," I told her, "even in a regular garage."

We both leaned against her car as the humid air blew across the parking lot, bringing with it a powerful dose of fumes from the busy pumping stations. We talked a bit more, just getting to know each other, when I realized that it was getting late. I told her that she should go ahead and get her car fixed, and I needed to get back on the road to deliver my berries. We decided that we would meet back up on my way back through town after I left New York.

On my return, I pulled over at the truck stop and was excited to find out how everything had gone with getting her car fixed. I had spoken to Suzi once because she had called my mom's house and left a message to call her at a pay phone at a designated time. That was in 1988 and I don't know how we were able to communicate without cell phones. I guess it was all we knew, but things are a lot easier now. I did know some wealthy folks back then who had the original "bag phones," but I had heard they caused many to get radiation burns on their ears from prolonged use. The rates at the time was about sixty cents a minute and just not affordable to the regular working man like me.

When I had talked to Suzi, she said she had not gotten the car fixed as of yet, but she had lined up a mechanic to look at the problem that evening. She said she missed me even though we had just met and was looking forward to seeing me again. It felt so good to hear those words. I wasted no time hurrying to get back to her with my truckload of brightly colored, empty plastic pallets. California did not allow the process of coloring plastic at the time due to the highly toxic chemicals and the toxic waste created by the process. I had picked up the pallets from a dirty old warehouse in Bayonne, New Jersey, a state that apparently allowed chemical use.

When I arrived at the truck stop, Suzi was in the same parking spot. She had acclimated herself to her new surroundings, using the restroom showers to clean up and keep her boys neat and tidy. I noticed that Jack had a new haircut and Derrick had a paddle ball play toy. I asked Suzi how everything went with the car. She said in a high-pitched voice, looking up at me with those beautiful blue eyes, "I kind of spent the money."

"You did?" I said, astonished. "On what?"

She went into this long, drawn-out explanation, almost coming to tears. "The kids were really getting tired of peanut butter sandwiches, and so we had some really nice meals in the restaurant. I bought some aspirin for my headache and had to get some tampons. Then Jack was looking like a hippie and Derrick wanted a toy to play with, so I bought him a paddle ball. It's hot at night and I can't run the car because it's broke and—"

"Stop, stop, stop," I said. "Okay so how much do you have left?

"It's all gone except for like $35," she whispered. I noticed her eyes were big and glassy. She hadn't looked like this when we'd first met. She had been very animated. I asked her about it and she told me she bought something else for the both of us if I wanted. Then she slowly pulled a little corner of a sandwich baggie from her purse. "It's this," she whispered as she showed me the white crystals in the corner of the plastic. "It's some of the purest, cleanest crank, straight from New Mexico," she said. Then she added, "I got it from a trucker who said it will help you on your runs."

I had tried this stuff in the past when I lived in Houston, Texas. I went on a couple of binges and slept for days afterward. I didn't care for it really. I enjoyed a joint once in a while when living in the country and loved to play guitar and sing about nature. "Suzi, really? Come on now, that money was to fix your car."

"I know, but I just needed a little pick-me-up. Let's go talk in your truck," she motioned. "Kids, Mommy's going to talk to Kraig in the truck."

"I want to go in the truck," they both yelled.

"Not right now. Later!"

Derrick yelled out, "You always have to have it your way."

"Derrick, don't make me get the belt! Play nice with Jack and both of you boys can get in the truck in just a little bit." We climbed up in the truck. I opened the passenger door for her and stood there while she negotiated the fuel tank steps in the wood clogs she wore. By the time she was pulling herself in the passenger seat, I got a bird's-eye view of her little ass cloaked in those tight hot pants. "And what are you looking at, sir?" she said with a smile.

"I'm looking at something every man would stare at if they were in my position."

"You ain't seen nothing yet, baby." Wow, this was really moving along quickly, I thought.

By the time I climbed into the driver's seat, she had four powdery rows strewn out on a little mirror from her purse. "Here, try a couple lines and lighten up already. I can get the car fixed. I just need a little more money. The mechanic said he could fix me up for $150 because he has an old motor just like mine at home. He said it needs a new stud, rocker arm, and pushrod."

I leaned over as she held the mirror of what looked like tiny shards of broken glass in four lines. I said, "Not here."

"Why not?" she said. "Don't be such a worry wart." She handed me a rolled-up dollar bill and I quickly snorted two lines. "Rocket fuel!" she exclaimed. "Feel the power!" Unlike the meth I had dabbled with in Houston provided by the Bandito's motorcycle gang whom I met at Cardi's Rock and Roll Club one night, this stuff had very little burn. "Just a dab will do ya," Suzi said in a semi-sinister tone. She pulled the small mirror up to her chin, cradling it in one hand and with the other she pulled the bill across the glass while snorting both lines at the same time, one in each nostril. "That's what I'm talking about," she said as she put the mirror back in her purse and simultaneously clutched her Kool 100 box and with her pink fingernails pulled a cigarette from the pack.

"I don't smoke in the truck," I said. "I don't really smoke anyways because it affects my singing voice. But now and again I'll smoke."

"Okay, Mr. Truck Driver," Suzi said. "How about this? Do you allow this in your truck?" Suzi dropped to her knees between the seats and pulled the lever that allowed my plush captain's chair seat to swivel and face her. I didn't think of it then, but now I'm pretty sure she had made her way around the inside of a truck in the past.

As the beautiful woman got down to business, I was ready to forget about the money and everything else. It felt new and exciting, just what I needed at the time. I couldn't believe how quickly things had moved along. I don't know if she had planned this or what, but I sure as hell wasn't questioning it. "You are a crazy girl," I said. Then I looked over at her kids, who were talking to a fat guy who had pulled up behind Suzi's car and trailer on a Harley Davidson. Her car was parked alongside the curb due to the parking spaces being for small cars. I was in the first truck parking space for big trucks just the other side of a curb.

"Your kids are talking to some guy, Suzi!" I sure as hell didn't want to interrupt her, but I felt like this was important.

She looked up quickly and sat back in relief. "Oh, that's Papa Smurf. He's the mechanic I was telling you about." Suzi gathered her things and glanced out to the passenger side-view mirror as she pulled her blonde hair back with her right hand. With her left, she removed the rubber band she was holding between her teeth and made a pony tail. I got up and made my way into the full-size stand-up sleeper of my 1987 Kenworth Aerodyne tractor to make myself presentable.

"Papa Smurf!" Suzi yelled while jumping out of the truck. All of a sudden, the innocent "I've never been in a truck" routine went right out the window. She ran over and gave this guy a hug. Then she grabbed a cigarette and quickly lit it, inhaling the first drag and letting the lit cig dangle from her lips while she put the lighter and pack of Kool 100s back in her purse. She continued to dangle her cigarette as she focused her attention on her son. "Jack, what have you got in your hair?" she asked as she dragged on the smoke and exhaled through her nose. Her hands were busy pulling apart Jack's strands of hair.

"Derrick put his gum in my hair," Jack cried out.

Derrick came to his own defense. "It was an accident, I went to throw it away and it landed in Jack's hair!"

"That's a lie, Mom, he did it on purpose," Jack said. He didn't seem too rattled about the gum that had clumped up his hair.

"Okay, boys, what did I tell you about this shit? We've got enough problems going on so just behave now," Suzi said as she took a long drag on the smoke and, for the first time since she lit it, pulled it from her mouth with her tanned fingers and pink-painted nails. After I got out of the truck and headed toward her, she motioned in my direction, "Papa Smurf, this is Kraig, the guy I told you about. Kraig, this is Papa Smurf. He's the mechanic and my friend now."

I put it together real fast that this is the guy who got her the party favors we had enjoyed earlier. "Glad to meet you, Papa Smurf."

"Papa is good enough," he mumbled, "or whatever."

"So, you can get the parts for her car?" I asked.

"Well, that's why I'm here. The engine I've got is not the same, but I've got a buddy that's got one just like hers and he'll take $35 bucks for the shit she needs."

"Okay and how much for you to fix it?" I asked.

He scratched his head and scrunched up his nose. "Well, I probably gotta get 100 bucks. I can get my tools from home and use my buddy's truck to come here and get her fixed up."

"Alright," I said, "I'll leave the money with the little lady, and when you get her up and running, she can pay you."

"Sounds like a plan," he said. "Can I get the $35 bucks for the parts and maybe $5 extra for gas?" I quickly handed him fifty bucks and told him to have a meal on me. He then mounted his Harley, kick started it, and rode off.

"See ya around, kids," he yelled as both boys gazed at the biker like he was a rock-n-roll Santa Claus.

By now the kids weren't interested in getting in the truck and I had a powerful craving for a cigarette myself. I went to the store and got Suzi a pack of Kool 100s and I bought a pack of Marlboro 100s for myself. Then I gave Suzi another $300 so she could pay Papa and have a little left over for food as well. We kissed a little and I jumped up in the big truck and drove off, waving good-bye to the three of them.

Work was the same routine. I delivered the plastic pallets to a manufacturing house in Los Angeles and drove north to Valencia where Points West Trucking was located. They processed my pay and gave me my next assignment. More berries for Hunts Point from Driscoll. This time they didn't have a full load so there was ten feet of empty space on the back of the trailer. This never happened. Most of the time every inch of the trailer was loaded. When I got on the road heading to NYC, I was dead tired. The lines I had done with Suzi kept me up for two days straight and now I was coming down. I was struggling to stay awake as I made my way east on I-10 out of Los Angeles. It's about 1,150 miles from Los Angeles to Big Spring, Texas, where Suzi was staying with her car. I was determined to make it back, but I had been awake for almost three days now just from those two little lines. I wanted some more, now.

Then I heard someone calling me over the CB radio. "Hey, Points West, you okay up there?" a rough voice said. I grabbed the CB handle, "Yeah, I'm okay, just a little tired is all." I was hitting the rumble strips along the side of the road now and again. Luckily, they were keeping me from falling asleep at the wheel. "I'm headed to Big Spring. Got a woman waiting on me there," I said in a slurred voice. "I could sure use some help if you know what I mean," I added, testing the waters to see if he might be an outlaw trucker with some of that same stuff Suzi had.

"Well, they call me Crossbow and I'm a headed to Springdale, Arkansas, to get me some more chickens to run out west." The man got my attention with the chicken talk since a lot of chicken haulers in their big, decked-out, fancy chicken trucks use something to keep them awake at night, I had heard. The man followed me, and we continued talking over the radio. He asked me about my girl and I told him about just meeting her recently but that I really liked her. We talked about all kinds of things as we cruised down the highway. It was 3:00 a.m. and we were about forty miles outside of El Paso, Texas. "Walking that dog and kicking that cat, chicken trucking is definitely where it's at, 10-4," he called on the CB. "Music Man," he said to me using my radio name, "I'm going to follow you into El Paso and there I got something that will keep you awake real good."

"Is it white?" I asked.

"Oh yeah," he said, "it's white and won't cost you a dime." I thanked him and we rolled into El Paso shortly thereafter. "Pull into this Petro at the next exit, Music Man." I did and we found a couple of parking spaces in the very back of the lot. We got out and shook hands. "Let's go get us a cup of coffee to start," the sixty-something-year-old, worn-out truck driver suggested. We got a booth and he went to the restroom. He grabbed about seven or eight packs of saltine crackers from the salad bar, and as he returned to our booth, he laid them on the table that separated us. "Here you go, Music Man. Just what the doctor ordered."

What's this guy talking about, I thought. "Here I go what?" I asked.

"Well, right there's the answer to your falling asleep at the wheel."

"Saltine crackers?"

"Yep," he said. "Why, you just crumble them crackers up and drop 'em in your underwear," he said with a strong Arkansas drawl. "You get them broken up and in your drawers and you can't even think about sleep. Why, you'll be itching and twitching all night long just wanting to get to where's you a-going so's you can get yourself cleaned up. Yep, they work real fine."

I thought a moment. "But you said you had the white stuff," I said while looking at him in disgust.

"They are white, and they are free!" he said.

I looked at him as I pushed the crackers aside on the table. "You've got to be shitting me."

Then he got to looking real serious at me, like he was mad and going to bust me up with his weathered fist. "Look at me, boy," he said in a stern voice. "That's right, it's a joke, but let me tell you this one thing: If I EVER catch you out here on the road looking for anything other than coffee to keep you awake, I'm a going to kick your ass wherever we are, so help me God!" I looked at him without saying a word. "I lost my son Johnny because of the shit you're looking for. He stayed up for days thinking he was going to make all this money in the trucking business by doing back-to-back-to-back long hauls with no sleep. He must have blacked out or something up there around Dagger City, Utah, because he drove through the guardrails coming through the pass, rode his truck to the bottom, and died when his rig erupted in a big fireball. It's not worth it, son. It's just not worth it!"

I could see the pain in his face as he sat there, allowing the story to take effect. Then Crossbow told me to get back in my truck and go to sleep before driving another mile. I nodded and did as he said. I was exhausted, and I realized that a quick fix was not the right thing to do. At that time, I couldn't imagine what it must have felt like for him to lose his son so needlessly. Then I realized that he had been talking to me on the CB all the way to El Paso to make sure I stayed alert, to keep me out of trouble. He went out of his way to make sure I arrived safely. Then he shared such a personal story that I was honestly touched by his concern. He did all of that for me, and I really appreciated it. It was like a guardian angel had guided me on the right path. I knew he was looking out for me and I appreciated the tough love. After that, whenever I drove a truck, I always remembered his words: "sleep or coffee and nothing more."

After I got a full, complete rest, I fueled up with diesel and headed for Big Spring, about 350 miles away, to see my girl. When I arrived, I found Suzi in the same spot. I parked my big rig close to her. After we kissed for a long time with the kids in the car, she told me another story as to why the car wasn't fixed and the money was gone. I said to her that I would fix her car if she agreed to come to New York and make a go at family life. I could be a father to her two boys and we could have children of our own. I was in the process of finding a house and some acreage and wanted to bring her into a stable home. Just like that, I was wanting to settle down with this girl. I'm not sure why I felt such a strong attraction, especially since she sure as hell couldn't be trusted with money, which was not a good sign. However, when I was with her, she said all the things I wanted to hear and did all the things I wanted her to do.

With that arrangement in place, I fixed her car and we emptied the U-Haul contents into the back of the trailer. That extra ten feet must have been a sign (the second one on that trip) and maybe that meant this was supposed to happen this way. I slid her bed's side rails and headboard on top of the Driscoll Berries, busting open the inflated bags that protected the delicate cargo. Clothes, toys, a stereo, a turntable, along with many boxes of dishes, and who knows what else. The back of the trailer was full and so was the walk-in sleeper. We returned the U-Haul to a nearby location and just left it there to be discovered in the morning. She had had the trailer for about six months past her contract and I wanted her to get rid of it right away. It was risky pulling it around. After that was taken care of, we headed to New York. Only one kid could fit in the truck cab at a time so I told Jack and Derrick they could take turns riding in the big truck with me.

I called my mom, who lived here in Owego, New York, and told her I was bringing my girlfriend and her kids to stay with her temporarily until I got back from delivering my berries in NYC. She said, "Then where's she going to live?"

I said, "Well, I was hoping she could stay at the lake house for a while until I get a job with Roger again."

My mom was not happy. "You mean my house on Cayuga Lake?"

I sighed a little. "Well, yeah, but it's only until I can get a local job with Roger again and buy a house."

She didn't know that I had already seen a nice little house on fourteen acres in Barton, New York, and kind of had it in my sights anyway. "You've got to be kidding me," she scolded. "You just met this woman at a truck stop two weeks ago and now you're moving her into my house? And from here she's moving to my lake house? You must be off your rocker. Does she have any money?"

"Well, not exactly, Mom. Actually, she's broke and I was hoping you could help out a little."

Mom answered quickly, "A little? You call that a little help? Give me a break! Who do I look like? Rockefeller?"

I knew then the answer was yes. She would do it. Whenever mom got sarcastic, she was going to be okay. I dropped Suzi and the kids off in Owego at Mom's house around midnight. I then went to meet my dad's old friend, Donny, in Little Meadows, Pennsylvania, a small town just across the border from New York and close to Apalachin. Donny had an old Chevy stake rack pickup that he called "Ole Blue." He met me in the Little Meadows Bank parking lot at 1:00 a.m. We loaded everything in his truck and I headed to Hunts Point to off-load my berries. Two days had passed since we had left Big Spring and a total of seven days since I had picked up the berries. That was way too much time for them to sit on a truck, especially for Driscoll. Due to the lateness and the produce that had gotten damaged during the move, I got into some trouble with my company. After they inspected the load, they decided that the entire crop had to go through the Hunts Point auction instead of being purchased by a reputable buyer. My company, Points West, would lose money on that delivery, and they didn't like to lose money. I knew I was on thin ice.

I ended up staying on with Points West for a bit longer. I needed to keep my job because I had asked Suzi to marry me and she'd said yes. I then asked my mom if she could watch the boys so we could go get married. She wasted no time in replying. "Hell no! Those kids are from Satan himself! Take them out of here and don't bring them back!" I asked my friend Tom if there was any way that he could help out. Fortunately, he and his wife, Katie, agreed to watch them while we were gone. I picked up Suzi two trips later and took her to Victorville, California, to the Out Post Wedding Chapel. No blood test required. Suzi's mom and her stepdad were there. I had asked Mom if she could come to the wedding, but she said it was too far of a trip to go to a wedding that was going to have only two other attendees plus the bride and groom. We got married and then headed to Hunts Point Market in the Bronx to make my scheduled delivery of berries. It wasn't the most romantic way to spend our "honeymoon," especially since we ended up in the rear parking lot of Hunts Point consummating our special day.

We delivered the berries successfully, but my company did not want me to leave the market until they knew where I was picking up my next load. Once that was sorted out, I finally got a dispatch and set off to Rochester, New York, for a full load of Ragu spaghetti sauce headed to Los Angeles. Suzi pleaded to stay on the truck so she could visit her mom and her sister. My buddy Tom and his wife didn't really want to watch the kids anymore and we were in a jam. Apparently, the kids had put soap in their aquarium and killed all the fish, and then both boys took a shit smack dab in the middle of the living room while Tom was taking a shower and Katie was at the store. They told me to just hurry and get back as soon as I could.

After returning from California, I was now a husband and father to two boys. I felt really good about my decision and it seemed like my life was finally moving in the direction I had always hoped it would. I bought that house on fourteen acres and moved in with the family. Things were great . . . until they weren't. We had birthday parties and cookouts, and I continued working for Roger. Suzi's mom came to visit and basically degraded me for buying her daughter used furniture. I had bought Suzi a nice antique dining room set. It was a claw-foot mahogany table with hand-carved chairs. I thought it was beautiful and Suzi seemed to like it too.

My mother-in-law told me if she were my wife that furniture would go in one door and out the other. I said, "I guess I'm glad you're not my wife." Well, that wasn't the right thing to say because that was followed by a huge fight. I threw some things around the house, a few of the chairs from the dining set as I recall. I tore the phone off the wall when her mom tried to call the cops. Then they both tried to leave in Suzi's car. I laid down behind the tire and told them they would have to run me over if they were going to leave. "Leave my wife here and you can go," I told my in-law. The kids were watching from their bedroom windows. They didn't scream or cry. Finally, she left and things seemed to subside for a while.

Once, I borrowed Suzi's car to get some parts for my Ford pickup. At first, she was hesitant to let me use it, but she finally gave in. While at the parts store parking lot, I rummaged around under the seats. I found a letter Suzi had written to her mom telling of a couple of joint bank accounts I had with my mom and she talked about my plans to buy a dump truck. I had to use a pencil to shade the paper to see the imprint of the words on the page that had been under the original letter. I returned home and made no reference to the discovery I had made. I just bought a couple of six packs of Bud and we drank long into the night, making mad passionate love into the wee hours of the morning.

About two weeks later, I left for work on a Saturday morning for half a day. I was supposed to be at work by 9:00 a.m., but I saw a yard sale just getting underway and I had to stop. There were some kids' toys on the lawn along with yard games like Jarts and a croquet set with the wooden balls and mallets. I felt the urge to buy something for the boys even though they had just been in trouble for having a water fight through the entire house. Derrick once again talked little brother Jack into trying to get him with the hose. Jack used it like a space ray gun and chased Derrick through the house, soaking everything in their path. When I asked Suzi about the mess, she told me what happened and that she told the boys if they ever do anything like that again they were going to be whipped with the belt. Anyway, after all of that I still wanted to get them something. I was having a tough time bonding with the boys for some reason. They were little devils for sure, but then again, I had been the same way growing up. I understood that it was mainly because of their unstable home life. Hell, they had been living at a truck stop for weeks. I didn't want to give up on them. Maybe finding some activities that we could do together would help build our relationship. I wanted my marriage to work and those kids were part of the deal.

I bought the yard games and even found a couple of bicycles too. When I got home, there was a car in my driveway that I had never seen before. "What the hell's going on here?" I asked as I walked into the kitchen from the back door. Suzi told me the kids were sleeping over at their friend's house, and it was just me, her, and "the Highway Man." The strange car belonged to the guy who worked for the highway department and had installed our drainpipe at the end of the driveway. Highway Man was sitting at my kitchen table with an open Budweiser. Suzi was working on her own beer at the counter by the sink.

Suzi said, "This is Bob, the guy who—"

"I know who he is," I interrupted. "What the hell is he doing here?" I looked at him and said, "Who the fuck do you think you are?" I pulled back and rammed a closed fist alongside his head and felt my fist go right through the sheet rock, punching a hole in the wall. I'm so glad I didn't hit a stud. "It's time for you to leave, Casanova." Suzi said he just stopped by to say hello. "Oh bullshit, Suzi, look at you wearing just my T-shirt and sweeping the kitchen floor. You haven't swept a floor since we've been married, you fucking whore!" I turned to Bob as he stood up, leaving his beer on the table. "Get the fuck out, you piece of shit!" I chased him out the back door as he ran around the corner of the house. I threw his full beer at him, missing him completely, but he saw it as it went whizzing by his head and landing in the yard with a thud. He hurried to his car, jumped in the driver's seat, and started the engine while locking his door at the same time. As he backed around to head down the driveway, I found a rake leaning against the side of the house and threw it at his car. He finally made it down the driveway and I went back inside.

Suzi had a cigarette by the time I got back to the kitchen. She was sitting at the kitchen table with a smug look on her face. "What is your problem? Nothin' was going on. He just stopped by to say hello."

Somehow I managed to keep my composure when all I really wanted to do was explode. I said as calmly as possible, "We need to go to counseling, Suzi." I was determined to make this marriage work. It had always been my goal to have a wife and family and I wasn't giving up without a fight. I told her that I had to get to work, but she asked me to stay home and make "mad passionate love to her." Hell, I couldn't turn that down. I called into work and told Roger I wasn't coming in that day. Suzi handed me a beer and we drank a couple and talked about who we could see for marriage counseling. She suggested Pastor John of the Lutheran church we attended. After we finished our third beer, we went to the bedroom. I knew this was basically makeup sex, but I thought that maybe after this fight things would improve. I had gotten a little out of hand, but I couldn't believe she had a random guy alone with her. Hopefully that was all water under the bridge now. She was in agreement about counseling, and I had hopes that she was willing to put in the work to make us a stronger family. I was prepared to devote everything I had to ensuring that my marriage didn't turn out the way my parents' had.

After a few weeks and one visit to Pastor John, I was sad to see that things didn't seem to be improving at all. We had a huge birthday party for Suzi. I thought making a big deal and showing her how important she was would help with our progress. Unfortunately, she got crazy drunk and brought both the ponies that I had gotten the kids into the kitchen. I'm not sure why she did that, unless it was to get attention, but I think maybe she was trying to get a reaction out of me, trying to provoke me. I knew better than that and I certainly never touched her.

Later that week, I came home after working a full day for Roger. It was about 4:30 in the afternoon and I was dog tired. When I pulled into the driveway, there was a Penske Rental truck and two other vehicles. One I recognized as Pastor John's. As I got out of the car, Pastor John was handing a box to a member of our church in the back of the truck. I recognized him as Bill from the men's Bible study group. "Pastor," I said calmly, "I would expect this from her, but never from you."

Then Suzi bounded out of the house and up to the truck announcing, "I'm leaving you, Kraig. I'm going to California with my kids!" I felt like I had started to bond with those boys and I don't think she liked that too much. We had been spending a lot of time out in the woods shooting BB guns and making forts from logs and branches. I felt like I couldn't win no matter what I did, and it was frustrating as hell.

I glanced into the back of the rental truck. "Well, first of all, that Snap-On tool chest is mine, and the pony saddles are too. The bed and that other stuff is hers, but that antique dresser and those boxes of Clarice Cliff dishes from Europe belonged to my grandma. None of that stuff is hers."

Playing mediator, the Pastor said, "Suzi?"

Suzi sighed and said, "Oh, well, he gave them to me, but just take them out if it makes him happy."

They continued to load stuff and I just got in my truck and didn't say a word. I went to my neighbor who I didn't really get along with because I had fired a warning shot into the air when I caught him cutting down some large oak trees on my property, but now I had an idea. I pulled into his driveway and pulled out a $100 bill. "I've got one more tree for you to cut down, and I'll pay you $100 to do it." I don't think he knew what to think, but he loved cutting down trees so I thought this would be perfect for him. He agreed to help and already had his chainsaw and gas in the back of his pickup truck. He followed me to the house and I showed him the huge old oak tree that had to be over one hundred years old. "Drop it," I told him. "It's not valuable, is it?"

He examined the tree. "Not really, just for firewood because it's just a yard tree and most likely has nails from treehouse steps and other metal things that have been hammered into it over the years. I notice those things because they will tear up a saw mill blade," he explained. That guy really loved trees.

I told him I wanted him to drop the tree so that it would fall across the driveway blocking Suzi in until I could get to my attorney's office on Monday to file some paperwork. I know it takes time for court papers to be processed, but this all made sense to me in that moment. I told the tree killer to wait a minute before he got started. Then I pulled the pastor aside and told him what my intentions were. I advised him that if he wanted to drive his car away in one piece, he should move it and his helper Bill's car, too, because a tree was coming down.

Suzi started screaming as the chainsaw coughed and sputtered to life. *Wanggg! Wanggg! Waaannggg!* Back and forth, the tree man sliced a wedge in the front of the mighty oak first. Then he went to the back side and cut at an angle, going down. It was cracking so loud and within minutes the tree hit the ground. I could feel the earth shake as the tree branches snapped and the trunk bounced on the grass. I just stood there staring at the mess because I couldn't believe what had happened. This huge oak was now lying *alongside* my driveway and not across it. The damn tree expert had screwed it up royally and totally missed the damn driveway!

Tree man said, "I was afraid that might happen. I suppose you want your money back." I thought back to how he never called the cops when I fired my

30-30 Winchester in his direction when he was snagging those trees in the woods. "No, it could have happened to anyone." He left, and Suzi continued to load her stuff and every now and again I had to point out what was mine. I tried to call the cops, but they told me she had lawful claim to everything we owned, and I should get an attorney. I hung up the phone and didn't tell Suzi what they had said since she probably already knew.

Suzi drove easily past the fallen oak tree, the branches scraping along the side of the rental truck as she gave me the finger. She even had her kids flip me off as they drove away. I knew she had to call from our phone to communicate with friends she would be visiting during her road trip. I went inside to find the phone bill with the numbers listed. It was gone so I called the phone company and they sent me a duplicate bill. I used it in the days that followed to try and track her down, often missing her as she drove to her next stop. "She was here for a night and took off for Cali," one woman told me. One guy said she had a flat tire in Pennsylvania at the start of her journey. She was down around Philadelphia. I called Penske rentals and they told me she rented the truck for a day to move from Barton, New York, to Waverly, about five miles down the road. They said they had contacted her and she told them she had gotten lost. Unbelievable. I finally found her at a number in Hanford, California. It was her brother who answered the phone. I said, "Let me talk to Suzi. This is her husband," as if I knew she was there.

He said, "Hey, I don't think she wants to talk to you, dude. Suzi!" he called out. "Your old man is on the phone!"

I asked her what her address was, and she declined to tell me. "You'll never find me in a million years, Kraig" and she hung up the phone.

I had been in touch with my attorney and all they needed was one day to finalize the annulment papers. We had only been married for six months and no children were born. I also contacted the Penske rental place again. They had a protocol they had to follow. When two weeks went by and the rental truck had not been returned, they reported it stolen. I got the license plate number and unit number, and told them she was in California. They didn't ask where or anything. They seemed pretty relaxed when it came to retrieving the truck. I then called the Kings County sheriff's office. "There is a stolen Penske truck at this phone number. I know you guys can reverse check and get the address."

"How do you know this truck is stolen, sir?" the dispatcher asked.

"It's my wife and I just talked to her at the number I gave you. The truck is stolen from New York."

"Okay, we will send a car by and check it out."

I was trying to keep her in one place so that I could arrange to have her served with the annulment papers. I called back about three hours later. The sheriff had run the phone number I gave them and had sent someone to the address. I heard that Suzi cried as they made her take everything out of the truck. I asked if they arrested her and they said no, that the Penske Corporation just wanted their truck back. They were not interested in prosecuting as it was simply a case of a broken contract and nothing more. She was granted permission to have the truck and just owed them more money. I was pissed. I wanted her to go to jail.

This feeling of needing to get revenge was nothing I learned in Bible study, that's for sure. I asked the sheriff's deputy who went out there if I could have the address and he said he couldn't provide me with that information. He then said he could tell me the towing company's name if I wanted that. I said yes that would be helpful and wrote down the address. It was some street in Riverdale, which is a small town south of Hanford. I called the towing company and said in a deep gruff voice, "Uh, yes, this is Roger Penske and I understand you have one of my trucks in your yard."

There was silence on the other end and then the man said, "Oh yes, Mr. Penske, we just dropped it in the back lot."

"Excellent and is the truck damaged at all?" I asked.

The young-sounding man said, "No sir, Mr. Penske, there are no dents at all and no broken glass."

I said, "Good, good, you did a great job and I thank you. Just one more thing. Can you tell me the address where you picked the unit up?" I heard papers rustling a little and he said the street name and number. "Thank you very much and have a fine day now!"

Two days later, the sheriff had the papers to serve with full payment in a money order as they required. I was told they went up to the front door and knocked. Then Suzi came to the door and didn't give any trouble as they served her the papers. "She thought I was there for a follow-up on the truck because she was surprised. Then she got upset when she understood that she was being served for the annulment," I was told.

I was glad that my attorney was able to get me an annulment for fraudulent inducement of a marriage, which was based on her having two other kids that she never told me about. I was free at last from this nightmare of a woman. I couldn't believe how fast I was married and then all of a sudden it was over. In the blink of an eye, I was single again. No wife, no family. We had so much fun together at the beginning that it just felt right. I felt like we were a good couple and that it would last for a long time. Of course, I guess I didn't see what I didn't want to see. She was a woman who liked things on her terms. I was sure that she would change, but that wasn't the case. The best thing to come out of that brief union was that it confirmed to me that I really wanted a family and a child of my own. I just wasn't sure it would ever happen.

About one and a half years later, I got served with court papers from Kings County Courthouse in Hanford, California. Suzi had a child and identified me as the father. I was shocked as hell that I had a kid that I didn't even know about. As soon as I could, I flew to the West Coast. First, I had to sign some papers and volunteer to have a blood sample taken. Apparently, my ex-wife was not exactly the loyal, monogamous type. That was fine by me because I would feel better if there was proof that I was the dad. Then we could deal with the rest.

I returned home and waited for the results. When I got the letter from the district attorney's office, I was scared to open it. What if I did have a child that I didn't know? What if I didn't? I wasn't sure how I would feel either way. Everything was moving so fast that I didn't really have time to think about it. I ripped the envelope open and saw that there was a 99.9 percent match. I was the father. I didn't waste one minute. I immediately sold everything I owned—dump trucks, tools, everything. Then I hitched up my twenty-three-foot Terry camper and began the journey from New York to California. It was hell pulling that camper with a short wheel–based Ford Bronco and no sway bars. Still, I was on a mission. I finally arrived in Kingsburg, California, and parked the camper at Riverland Resort on Highway 99 just south of Fresno.

In the morning, I would meet my child.

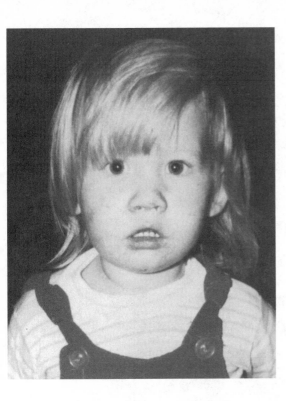

Rob as a toddler.

When I got custody of my son.

Rob's first visit to California.

Like father, like son.

At Yosemite National Park.

The teen years.

My ex-wife, Jo-an, with Rob on graduation day.

A fine young man.

The Trump Troubadour. Ronald Evans Photography, Binghamton, New York.

"When you go through deep waters, I will be with you." Isaiah 43:2. Ronald Evans Photography, Binghamton, New York.

6

THE HIGHWAY SEEMS TO BE MY ONLY HOME

By February 2016, I was heavily invested in my mission to get Donald Trump elected first as the Republican Party candidate and then the president of the United States. I could visualize it happening, but I realized that it would take people like me, regular folks on the ground delivering his message of a new America, to make it happen. For the first time in my life, I felt a real connection with a politician, and after what I had been through with my son, I now had the time and energy to dedicate to the campaign.

This time it was just me, with Rob's urn by my side. I made my own schedule and did things the way I wanted to do them. There was a growing list of Trump rallies being announced and more added every week. Keeping up was a daunting task, but I felt like I could get to most of them, even the ones on the West Coast. After Donald Trump had stood up on that stage and promised that he would help with this horrible epidemic that had stolen my son from me, I had renewed energy and focus.

I thought about how the rallies in Iowa had gone and how I wanted to do things differently this time. Attending those early campaign events educated me on what it was like to be part of a political machine. I had great memories of those cities—Des Moines, Cedar Falls, Sioux Center, and most of all the Urbandale rally where Mr. Trump had made that promise to me in front of the 2,500 or so attendees. He also told the crowd, while pointing to me, that

I was a good father. Every time I thought about that, it made me feel happy inside. It made me feel special. I was ready to set out on my own.

I went home briefly to recuperate. I told a few friends that I was resting up and then hitting the road for more rallies. They all enjoyed the Trump lawn signs I'd brought back from the North Charleston rally. I helped myself to over half of them and felt like Santa Claus passing them out to Trump supporters here at home in Owego. The rallies in Myrtle Beach, Pawleys Island, and North Charleston, South Carolina, were somewhat uneventful. There was always talk in the media about possible violence breaking out, but I hadn't seen that, so I felt safe venturing on to more rallies. As I looked on the Trump website, I saw that the Radford, Virginia, rally was scheduled for Monday, February 29, at noon.

I set off for the Trump rally at Radford University in southwest Virginia. The day after that event was Super Tuesday. As far as I could figure, Super Tuesday is really just a little precursor to the main election. A bunch of states get together and determine if they will have a caucus, primary, or state election. It lets people know what their fellow state residents are thinking. I stayed at the Super 8 in Christiansburg just outside of Radford. The day started early for me. It was about 6:00 a.m. and I had already secured a parking spot by 6:30. As always, I wanted to get pretty close to the main doors.

I grabbed my guitar and walked to the entrance. There were about thirty people already sitting and standing in a jagged line by the doors. I asked the sitters what they would do with their chairs once the doors opened and they all told me they would just leave them outside against the building. If someone took them, they didn't care. They considered it the cost of admission since most of the rallies were giving out free tickets. I do remember that there was a $25 entry fee in Bismarck, North Dakota, but that rally was in conjunction with the Oil and Gas Industry Trade Show and Convention. Trump was basically a guest speaker and anyone who wanted to hear Mr. Trump had to buy a ticket to the convention.

At Radford, I got situated and played a bunch of songs for the folks at the head of the line. The crowd remained small initially, but then all of a sudden, they started coming out of the woodwork. What was once a nice little line became a herd of people crowding the entrance doors, fifteen to twenty people wide and one hundred or so deep. The crowd twisted down the sidewalk and around the parking lot twice. Then it circled around the back lot three times with thousands of hopefuls clamoring to see their candidate, Mr. Donald J. Trump. I continued playing from my rapidly growing catalog of Trump songs along with some old country and my original tunes. I noticed once again, as I had in South Carolina, lots of smokers—young and old—smokers of all ages puffing on every brand of cigarette on the market. Most were students, it seemed, and apparently they hadn't heard about the hazards of smoking. Parents were lighting up and handing a cigarette to their teenage son or daughter. I just wasn't used to so many smokers and it caught me off guard.

Outside, things didn't get too wild with protesters. There was a group that sprung up seemingly out of nowhere and started chanting, "No more hate! No more hate!" Cops quickly escorted them to an area far away from the Trump supporters standing in line to see the rally. As I walked up and down the line, I'd ask, "Hey, who wants to hear a Trump song?" If the people directly in ear shot mumbled, "No, that's okay," I would immediately tag them as possible incognito Trump protesters.

"Are you getting ready to disrupt the rally?" I asked one guy.

"Why do you say that?" he asked. I explained that everyone who supported Trump would jump at the chance to hear a Trump song. "Well, we're undecided, that's why we're here."

I knew this to be true as many folks that came to the rallies were undecided, but most were bona fide Trump supporters after they had heard the mesmerizing speeches from the presidential candidate. At 10:00 a.m., the doors opened and hordes of people began steadily moving forward. It was slow going at first since everyone had to empty their pockets, walk through a metal detector, and be scanned by a handheld wand. Outside of these rallies, it continued to become more and more circus-like. Vendors everywhere were pulling wagons, carrying bags and stacks of $3 hats (and selling them for $20), $5 T-shirts going for $25–$35 and some as much as $50 depending on how much print was on them.

A couple of hours before the event started, I met a vendor called Whitey, named aptly due to his thick shock of white hair and matching mustache. He was a racetrack promoter from Virginia and he told me that he couldn't pass up the opportunity to make some easy money. He brought 200 T-shirts that he had created, which read, "Finally someone with balls." He sold them all for $20 and was cleaned out before the rally started at noon. I ended up running into Whitey at many rallies since he was clearly not going to let these financial opportunities pass him by.

Once noon arrived, a huge screen was placed strategically in the center of the yard with a clear view for everyone. That screen had to be twenty feet wide and maybe fifteen feet tall and there were huge speakers placed strategically around the property. Thousands of people still circled the parking lot. The crowd at the front door was now pushing and shoving to try and squeeze their way into the auditorium. And then, without warning, the doors were slammed closed and locked.

Just then, the big screen TV flickered to life, and front and center was a preacher man at the podium speaking from inside the building. He didn't open with prayer like one might expect. The invocation came after a loud and angry voice screaming into the microphone. "I'm tired of illegal immigrants getting better health coverage provided by Americans than our own troops that risk their lives for our country!" When this blasted through the outside speakers, the crowd erupted right on cue. The thousands of supporters that twisted around the parking lot broke into a dead run toward the front doors to get closer to the screen. "I'm tired of illegals taking our jobs or not working and making us pay for their housing and families!" Again, the crowd roared with agreement. "I'm tired of Americans being tagged second most important. This is our country and we need to make a stand! We're not going to let the government take away our guns, are we?" The crowd roared once again and the thousands of supporters in line were now corralled around the big screen, clapping and cheering. "Let us pray," the preacher said in a much calmer and more serene voice as if whispering to God himself. It was a powerful moment to witness, I must say. And with all the people cheering on this man, it was clear that he was striking a chord with many who had felt previously unheard.

A few protesters made it inside, and when they revealed themselves, they were promptly escorted from the Dedmon Center. Trump called out to the crowd and instructed them to "not hurt or touch the protesters" and "if you see a bad egg, just point them out and we will kick them out of this gathering." The big news of the day was when a photojournalist tried to get to an area where some protesters were being confronted and the Secret Service staff grabbed him on the shoulder. Somehow the photographer fell to the floor and the officials put him in a chokehold, pressing his head to the ground. The photographer started kicking hard and the altercation escalated into a major disruption. Things finally calmed down, and after the rally, I knew it was time to hit the road.

Next, I was headed to Columbus, Ohio. On the way, I picked up an older man who was hitchhiking. I had decided to take a more rural route to avoid traffic and there he was standing all alone. I noticed his 101st Airborne US Army hat, and I asked where he was headed. He said just down the road about sixty miles, then south about forty-five minutes. I made room in the front seat for him and put his belongings, which fit into a gunny sack, into the back of my pickup. "I'm going to visit a friend of mine from the Army. He's been sick the last two months and I want to see him."

I told him I could get him through the first leg of his trip, but would have to keep heading to Columbus. He said that would be fine. We got to the small town and he asked me if I could spare a few bucks. I asked him if he was hungry and he said he hadn't eaten since breakfast. I pulled into a KFC and we feasted after a quick prayer. His name was John and he was an interesting character. I convinced him to get a room that I would pay for and then he could start out fresh in the morning. Lord knows he could have used a good night's sleep, and a bath wouldn't hurt him none either.

I got him to a motel and signed him in. "Do you give veteran discounts here?" I asked.

"No sir, we do not," the man behind the counter replied.

"How about trucker's discount with a CDL?" I tried again.

He said, "Yes, truckers can have a room, one night for $49 plus tax." A man who signs his name on the dotted line and says he will risk his life for our country can't get a measly discount on a room, but a guy who drives a truck and delivers toilet paper can? It just doesn't make sense.

I paid for the room and bought John a few things at the store and gave him $40 cash. We shook hands and he thanked me. This was a moment I will always remember from my journey because even though I was certainly not a rich man, I didn't hesitate to share what I had with this guy who was down on his luck. It felt really good to make a difference in someone's life. It helped to solidify that I was doing the right thing.

The Columbus rally took place on February 26, Super Tuesday, and was for the most part uneventful. Not a lot of protesters attended and the ones that did show up were surprisingly peaceful. I saw Whitey again and he was fully restocked with his shirts. Not only that, but this time he had jacked up his prices. I guess it was the law of supply and demand. During this rally, Trump basically called out one of his opponents—Ohio governor John Kasich—and told him if it weren't for the gas and oil industry in Ohio, the state would be "bankrupt." I heard about this outside. I didn't go inside this rally. In fact, I didn't need to go inside many of them because the scene played out almost note for note each time. Trump would make all kinds of proclamations and the crowd would cheer and boo, whichever response Trump was seeking at the time.

The next rally was on March 1 in Louisville, Kentucky, and it was again pretty much uneventful outside. I didn't go inside this time either and later I heard about Trump getting the crowd riled up when some protesters appeared. "Get them out of here!" he had chanted.

The March 7 rally was at the Cabarrus Arena and Events Center in Concord, North Carolina, at noon. There, I met so many nice people and shared Rob's story to many more. They were so welcoming and receptive that it felt really good. I played the guitar and sang until I was hoarse. Such wonderful people came to most of the rallies, but for some reason, this time the folks just made me laugh. I told them I was from New York and you would have thought I'd committed a sin. One group asked me if I was a "half-back Yankee."

I said, "Well, I'm not sure what that is."

The spokesperson for the group said, "A half-back Yankee is a Yankee that moves to Florida, finds out it's too hot, and heads back north till he gets to the perfect weather here in North Carolina and he ends up calling it home. Then you've got a half-back Yankee!" I said not to worry because I was just passing through. He said, "Oh, I guess that'll be okay then. Hey, play me some ole Hank if you can."

I played three Hank Williams tunes and moved on to the next group of supporters. It was these folks and thousands more just like them that made the rallies the fulfilling experiences that they were. It made me feel like I had a purpose, a reason for going on. Their encouragement made me want to get out there and talk to everyone I could about the dangers of heroin and how it can be devastating not only to the user, but also for those left behind.

Soon I was getting hugs and warm embraces from many who said they had a family member or friend who had died from this horrific drug. Some even confessed that they were also addicts and tried to explain to me how hard it was to kick the habit. They confided that if an addict is faced with the decision to get clean or get another bag of dope, they would most certainly go with the latter. The addicts all seemed to agree that they would need someone to encourage them to get clean. They couldn't do it alone. It could be a child, husband, wife, sister, anyone. It was just important that someone be with them and let them know they were loved and cared for. It broke my heart to hear these stories. It just astounded me that no matter where I went it seemed that this epidemic had its deadly grip on the population, and most were regular, hard-working folks like me.

The next stop on the Trump Trail was Fayetteville, North Carolina, at the Crown Center Arena, which held about ten thousand people. I could see that the venues were increasing in size to keep up with the ever-growing crowds demanding entry to the hottest ticket in town. This rally started at 7:00 p.m. with doors opening at 5:00. The vendors and protesters alike were restricted to the sidewalk around the perimeter. Any place on the actual grounds was off-limits as Trump rented the entire facility and demanded that no vendors or protesters be allowed on the rented space. In the beginning, Mr. Trump didn't say anything about the vendors selling shirts, hats, buttons, flags, and anything you can imagine with "Trump" printed on them.

However, the Trump campaign soon started selling their own merchandise, but only offered the items online. The vendors would flock to the rallies by the hundreds to cash in on his name. In Iowa it was mittens, wool hats, and scarves during the month of January. Now the focus was on hats, T-shirts, and Trump flags. The vendors would chant to the passing crowds just like they were at a carnival or state fair, selling two hundred hats at $20 for a cool $4,000. The cost was about $2.50–$3.00 each, making the profit margin equivalent to a drug dealer's profit.

My old pal Whitey continued to set up his booth and sell his wares. He made sure to cover every rally city on the East Coast. He had an especially large operation in Pigeon Forge, Tennessee. He told me that he was generating thousands of dollars a day from that merchandise. That entrepreneurial guy even set up at a gas station parking lot in Washington, Pennsylvania, a border town to West Virginia, just outside of Wheeling. He never asked permission to do it. He just pulled up and started unloading. At that gas station, he said the manager told him he didn't have authorization to do that. Whitey said that he shouldn't mind since it was for a good cause. The manager apparently called his boss, who asked how business was going. When the manager told him they were swamped, the owner said to give Whitey some free coffee and let him and his crew stay for as long as they wanted. Whitey sent a crew to the station every day after that.

Back in Fayetteville, things got very exciting. There were high school cheerleaders, college kids, adults, and even toddlers coming to see Trump. There were literally thousands of people attending this gala, and this was another occasion where people who had heard my story were coming up to me either offering encouragement or sharing a sad addiction story of their own. Sometimes I wasn't sure what I was more surprised by—how hugely popular Donald Trump and his rallies had become or how this horrible epidemic had touched every single community in this country. Before the tragedy with Rob, I never had any idea how widespread this problem really was. It had been heartbreaking to learn the truth.

This rally also was one of the first places where a protester who was removed from the event was sucker-punched while he was being escorted out of the arena. This drew a tremendous amount of coverage as it was really the first time that campaign violence was shown on national TV, and that meant it was shown over and over. The media was eager to cover this kind of stuff because at every rally, Trump never failed to refer to the media as "scum" and "bad people," often prompting the supporters to boo the media on cue to validate his point.

The next stop was St. Louis, Missouri, on March 11 at the Peabody Opera House. A couple hundred protesters outside provoked thousands of Trump supporters who couldn't make it into the rally due to capacity restrictions. One protester stomped and ground on the American flag with his work boots, which prompted supporters to retaliate. Another man confronted him, and it started getting ugly. A group of veterans also had their say with the protester and several were arrested because fists were swinging, and things quickly escalated. The trouble started because of the way this rally was set up. Those attending had to file past the gauntlet of protesters, making for an inevitable confrontation. As the Trump crowds grew, so did the number of protesters, and this time they were on either side of the path taunting the supporters with megaphones and signs.

Despite those challenges, I did meet some very nice folks and also made a lifelong friendship with a guy named Michael, who was there with his wife. They were fun to talk to and they really enjoyed the music I played for them. They especially liked how I played "Amazing Grace" when that fight broke out. We have remained friends even though he doesn't like my harsh words against our president now. Later that evening, the rally scheduled for Chicago was canceled after hundreds of protesters had already lined up at the venue amid violent scuffles.

Dayton, Ohio, was a particularly fun rally to attend, but there was one strange incident. I had a heroin addict come to me after I played "Cherished Memories." The addict had obviously just used recently because she was moving slowly, slurring her words, and acting loopy. She reminded me of a minstrel or a fairy-tale storyteller. "You didn't understand your son's needs," she told me after hearing the song. "You didn't listen to his needs. Your son needed you to love him. I know because my mom doesn't understand me either. My father doesn't even want to visit me. You should have listened to your son, that's what I think. He just wanted to be held and you just didn't see that. I'm not saying it's your fault because parents usually just don't understand." I didn't respond. I just listened. I thought that was exactly what she needed, someone to listen to her. Then I watched as she sat on a bench along the sidewalk and slumped down as her head nodded forward. Unfortunately, I either heard stories like this or witnessed it in person after people heard about me losing Rob. It was painful for me to see a real-life example of how bad things were in this country.

The next rally was scheduled for March 13 in Boca Raton. I was excited because that meant I could swing by and visit my good friends, Pastor Mark and his wonderful wife, Ms. Debbie, at the cowboy church in Florida. I first stopped at the church grounds and visited with all my friends there. I arrived on a Friday and stayed the weekend, going to both Sunday services on the 13th. I played my Christian songs and experienced the same emotions I always have after visiting this church, a very warm and content feeling that can only be described as peaceful and serene.

The rally in Boca Raton was scheduled to start that night at 7:00, and I hit the road soon after the second service. I was headed for the Sunset Cove Amphitheater. Being early spring, the weather was clear, the sun was bright, and I was feeling refreshed after visiting the church. I was excited for this sunny outdoor event. As usual, I wanted to arrive promptly, and I got to Boca around 3:00. There was already a line, and they were starting to let folks in a little early, taking time once again to pass through the metal detectors and the scanning by the Secret Service. It was interesting to watch as the crowds continued to get bigger and lines formed earlier and earlier for each rally. I knew I was witnessing a true groundswell of support for a politician, something that hadn't happened in our country for a long time. Regardless of party affiliation, it was truly inspiring to see people so invested and willing to participate. As I was playing my songs on my Martin guitar with Trump stickers affixed, I heard a familiar voice from afar. It was a man I had met in Iowa who worked for *Financial Times* magazine.

He ran up to me. "Hey, Kraig, remember me? My name is Demetri. We met in Iowa at the Ames rally."

I had talked to so many media people that they did start to blend together, but I remembered this fellow because he had shown so much interest in my son and had asked me so many questions regarding his life. It really made an impact on me.

"Of course, I remember you! It's nice our paths have crossed once again," I said.

We chatted for a short while and he asked me to sing my newest song, "Trump Train." Without missing a beat, I launched into it, giving him and the other gathering supporters a heartfelt, spirited performance. I was so into it that during my hard strumming I broke a string, but being a professional, I just kept on playing. After the song, everyone applauded and hollered their approval.

Then the reporter pulled me aside to talk. "I don't know how you kept on playing and didn't miss a beat," he told me.

"Well, I guess I need some new strings," I responded.

"Hey, Kraig, I've got to get inside, but I want to get together and do a piece on you. I'll be in touch. Is your number still the same?" he asked.

"Yep, just give me a call."

"Okay, will do, friend. Got to run," he said as he made his way to the entrance of the outdoor facility. I didn't give that news article much credence. I'd heard a lot of promises about news coverage at each rally. Sometimes they came through and sometimes they didn't. I had learned to just wait and see.

Well, later on the campaign trail, I was asked to meet with a photographer for some photos that were used in a pretty good-sized article about me and my mission. It was exciting and inspirational.

Outdoor rallies were a totally different animal because it was a security nightmare from what I was told by a couple agents I had gotten to know from the other events. It seemed the security teams didn't switch members until somewhere west of Indiana. Then another security group took over. The problem with outdoor events was ultralights and other types of small planes. The ultralights were common along the shoreline where it was more difficult to secure no-fly zones. It took some time before the rally could be locked down and signed-off as safe for candidate Trump to come onstage and speak.

After my photographer friend went into the facility, I heard a few other familiar voices coming from the crowd. It turned out to be more journalists that I had met along the way. There was a group of Swedish news people who I had first connected with in North Charleston, South Carolina. We talked briefly, and they too had to enter the facility to stake out their place near the stage, if possible. They indicated that they would contact me later for an on-camera interview at my home in Owego to be shown on Swedish Channel 4.

While playing for the supporters waiting in line to enter a Florida rally, I noticed a woman standing alone and listening to me play and talk about Rob. After a few songs, the line moved along, and she walked up to me and asked if I was a part of the Trump campaign. A lot of people asked that question during my travels. I said, "No, I only wish I were getting a paycheck to help with the expenses, but I'm doing this for much more than money. For me it's all about having a purpose in life. To wake up and have meaning is very important to me. My mission is telling my son Rob's story and talking to people about the ongoing heroin epidemic we have found ourselves in. By the way, what's your name?"

She responded in a quiet and somewhat shy voice, "My name is Janet and I lost my son Tommy last year to the same stuff your son died of. Heroin mixed with fentanyl."

I reached out and held her close to my chest, now crying myself as she sobbed softly. Then I set my guitar down in the case that had been left open on the sidewalk in hopes that supporters would drop a dollar bill or two in there while standing in line. I continued to hold the heartbroken mother in my arms. "Oh, Janet, I'm so sorry," I told her. "Parents are not supposed to bury their children. It's just so hard to understand and live with."

The woman was crying and trying to talk, but she was just too emotional to get anything out. She clutched my shirt sleeves and pulled back. She finally said, "You have to keep telling your story. I hope Mr. Trump can stop this madness."

I nodded in agreement. "I hope that somehow I can make a difference," I told her. "Do you have anybody you can talk to and be with? I have found singing to the supporters gives me peace of mind, but that doesn't help you any."

She pulled back and wiped the tears from her eyes, still halfway sobbing, she said, "Maybe I should go to the rallies with you, but I can't sing very well." That made us both laugh a little and helped to lighten the mood. Then she turned serious again. "My other son, Jim, is into the same stuff and he just won't listen to me. I know he's in the same trap that Tommy was in."

I tried to comfort her as much as possible. "All we can do as parents is point our kids in the direction we would like them to go. It's up to them which direction they actually choose. We automatically want to blame ourselves, thinking we failed somehow as parents. You're lucky you have another child. I wish I had any kind of family to focus on. My advice would be to not give up on Jim. You make sure you're there for him with support and love, okay?"

She nodded and said, "God Bless you, Mr. Moss."

I told her to be strong and everything will be okay. Somehow everything will work out. "I'm not sure how," I said, "but it will."

This kind of exchange became increasingly common, unfortunately, because there were so many suffering. At first, I was taken aback and not sure how to respond. The emotions of pain and grief were so very personal that I wanted to respect their grieving process. However, I did become adept at providing comfort and giving them as much hope as possible. This was when it felt like I was actually making a difference. I knew I was helping the Trump campaign with my media appearances as my profile continued to grow, but it was moments like this that really gave me satisfaction. It helped to validate that I was doing the right thing, that there was a reason for me to take on this mission. I wasn't sure if I would be able to help, but this, and other situations just like it, gave me the energy and motivation to continue. I was actually making a difference in the lives of these nice people who didn't know me from

Adam. I think that sometimes, in the heat of the moment, we make promises out of desperation but often don't follow up. There were a lot of things in my life that I screwed up, but this time, I was sticking to my word and honoring my son. I was making a difference and helping those who were suffering from the indescribable pain that I had endured. It felt good to keep my promise to my son. I knew he would have been proud.

I took off from the Florida rally at 6:00, one hour before it was scheduled to start. I had to drive fast to make it to the next one in Hickory, North Carolina, some 780 miles away. I drove fast and hard, and barely escaped a few speeding tickets along the way. I stopped only for gas and grabbed a sandwich during fueling. I arrived at the Lenoir-Rhyne University in Hickory almost twelve hours later, at 6:00 a.m. I had driven through the night and was tired as a worn-out shoe, but when I saw the thousands of supporters already standing in line, I was rejuvenated. A few folks called out, "Hey, Trump Troubadour, sing us a Trump song!" Man, those news stories must have really been making the rounds! I sang a few songs and posed for some photo ops, even a few with toddlers in strollers. There were a lot of protesters at this rally. Apparently, there were a lot of rabble-rousers mixed in because I later found out that many got into the event only to be escorted out after making it clear that their intention was to disrupt the festivities.

One thing I noticed outside with the majority of the protesters was that although they were large in numbers and very loud at times, they were not aggressive or unruly. I commented to one of the leaders that I was very impressed as to how they were getting their message across and not creating a violent scene. We talked for a while and then I went back to performing. I played "Amazing Grace" and a couple of my Christian songs. I was so tired by this time. The exhaustion from the overnight drive had caught up to me. Also, playing songs and talking with people was very rewarding, but that was tiring as well. I was ready for a little break.

It was March 14, my sister's birthday, and I decided to relax a bit and give her a call. She was living in Seattle and we tried to keep in touch as much as we could. After I wished her a happy birthday, she told me that she had seen me on the news now and again and she was having some trouble with her friends when they found out I was her brother. They hated Trump and somehow took that anger out on her, as if it was her fault that I supported Trump. My sister told me she was even occasionally wearing a scarf around her face to keep a low profile. I thought she was overdoing it, but that was up to her. The memories of my childhood mistreatment of her never seemed to leave her, and I guess I understood. It was just kid stuff for me, but she took some things very seriously. Even though it was usually unspoken between us, I felt so horrible that I had not been the big brother she had deserved. I just hoped I could make it up to her.

I had a break in my rally schedule and I went home to Owego for a while. I spent my days with my good friend Roger and relived my experiences on the road. He was pretty much in tune with everything as I called him practically every day and told him about my adventures on the road. Roger talked to me for a long time, often through the night, as I drove from one rally to the next and one state to another. He would keep me awake by listening and making me laugh when I needed it the most. I was happy to have him as a part of my life.

I didn't have time to get too comfortable. The next rally was held at the Janesville Holiday Express Conference Center in Wisconsin, which was a twelve-hour drive from home. I stayed at the hotel and the next morning about fifty protesters had taken over the lobby. "Love Trumps Hate!" "Love Trumps Hate!" they were chanting. Ten people had even somehow handcuffed themselves together and had their arms inside a six-inch PVC pipe. The handcuffs were inside the tubes and there was no way for the local police to get to them. There were about a dozen officers in the lobby along with media and the energetic protesters. The police realized the difficulty of arresting this group, but also couldn't get them to disperse. It was basically a standoff. Regardless, I was still hungry from my trip, so I fixed some toast and a bowl of cereal.

Outside, the scene was a familiar one. There were thousands of folks lined up for the town hall. I noticed a few protesters huddling up and then I saw a dude I recognized from the St. Louis rally. I walked up to him and said, "Hey, I remember you from St. Louis. How you doing?"

He was a regular type of guy, black, about thirty years old. He said, "Yeah, I remember you, too. Well, we are getting paid to come to rallies and stir up some shit. Look up there." The man pointed to the rooftop of the Holiday Inn. There were at least five men in uniform holding what looked like AK-47s and one of them was looking through binoculars. "They're going to keep us down today with that kind of stuff."

"How much you getting paid, man?" I asked.

"I'm getting $500 for this rally, but I got some friends to come, and so I get extra for that. Some dudes are getting a grand and even more if they turn it upside down. Not sure who's paying us, and I don't really care. I need the money."

"How did you get here?"

"A bus," he told me. "The group we belong to paid for a bus to get us here. Why do you like that racist Trump asshole anyway?"

I said, "He wants to help drug addicts get clean and help stop the heroin problem we have in this country."

"He ain't going to do shit, man, you wait and see. He ain't going to do shit."

I met some other nice folks at that event. One girl had her friend with her and they both listened intently as I talked about heroin and the big problems it can cause. Spreading the word about the crisis always made me feel like the trip had been worth it. If I could just reach a few folks in each state, I was at least touching lives.

The next day, Appleton, Wisconsin, was on the schedule. I took off once again, leaving the thousands of supporters, all probably wishing they had gotten there earlier so they would have made it inside. The venues had clearly been obtained in advance. It was obvious that they hadn't planned on such a large number of supporters at these rallies, and they were still growing.

I stayed at the Appleton Radisson Hotel to take advantage of the parking. The rooms were expensive, but it was worth it. Inside the hotel, I met some media folks from CNN, ABC, MSNBC, and others who I had talked to at some of the previous rallies. It was almost like we were all members of the same club, running into each other at different events without any preplanning. After breakfast, I went outside to entertain the six-thousand-plus supporters eagerly waiting in line to jockey for space in this one-thousand-seat venue. I'm not exaggerating when I say the line went around the block and as far as the eye could see. I moved along the group as fast as I could, playing for everyone. I met some more of those Bernie Sanders supporters that had started showing up. This time there was another guy with a guitar. We agreed to play a couple of tunes together. I promised that I wouldn't play any Trump songs and he wouldn't play any Bernie songs, if there were any. This was the largest gathering of Bernie people that I had encountered, at least 150 or so. They stayed across the street and held signs that read "Love Not Hate" and

"Trump's a Racist." I had the most fun when I was playing "Trump Train" and a supporter standing in line joined in and sang along.

Next, I had to retrace my steps and head back to New York; this time Rochester was the next stop on the Trump Trail, but I wasn't as motivated because that rally didn't take place until April 10, a few weeks after the ones in Wisconsin. There had been a break in the schedule and I was sitting idle, hanging around at home and talking with Roger. This rally location was the Jet Smart aviation hanger at 3:00 p.m. There were lots of very nice folks in attendance. I also made appearances at the other New York events, one in Rome and the other in Watertown. However, I was feeling a little depressed and unmotivated.

April 7, 2016, would have been Rob's twenty-seventh birthday and I hadn't realized how hard it would hit me. With that break in the rally schedule, I had time to think about him and it was tough. I felt like I had entered into some kind of depression. I just had no desire to do anything, didn't even care if I woke up the next morning. I was just so alone that I felt truly lost.

I decided to sit in Rob's bedroom, which hadn't been touched since he died. I looked around his room to see the things that were important to him. I tried to imagine what he saw when he looked around here. There was a picture of him and me. It was held up against the back of a shelf on his bookstand. There was no frame and it was beginning to roll up from the weight of the 8 × 11 photo. There were also things he had gathered from some of our outings. A race-day pass from the California 500 we attended while living out West. A snapshot of us taken at the house in Coarsegold with both of us wearing our pink shirts, jeans, and ostrich quill boots. It dawned on me there wasn't a single picture of his real mom, Suzi, or any of my second or third wife. Just him and me doing things together. The reality of my situation hit me so hard, and all at once. My son was gone forever.

I cried and asked God to help me make it through these tough times, to somehow give me purpose or show me the way He wanted me to go. I was a wreck. Just so out of control with emotion and sadness. I pulled one of Rob's yearbooks from his shelf and flipped through it. By chance, I noticed a file folder sticking out from the pages that read "Find me" on the little portion that was visible. I was curious so I opened the yearbook and began reading.

I love you. I love my whole family with my whole heart. If you're finding this, I'm either dead or in jail. If dead, send my PS3 and all my games to Jack, my brother, along with my other brother's glove and zippo. I have them put up. Also let my mother, sisters, and cousins pick through my clothes and my other posetions [possessions] and let them have a few items. My vase I made is at Mary's Tattoo Shop. She can have it so leave her alone. But my father, above all, can pick what he wants to remember me by. Don't be a dick, Dad! (Love you.) Also drink beers and fucking live happy lives and fuck the haters and fish. So bearing that in mind I just didn't want to deal w/my life/bullshit anymore.

Later

Love always

Rob J. Moss Rob J. Moss

PS. I want cremation. Do a viewing then cremate My Ass and have me split up between my Mothers and father.

He had signed it "Rob J. Moss," twice. The first one was sloppy and the next one much neater.

I was devastated. It was a suicide note combined with a last will and testament. He was signing off from this world. He was saying good-bye. He knew the end was imminent and that broke my heart. I could hardly believe it, and I hadn't found it until two years after he passed. While his death was surely an accidental overdose, it appeared that he was aware that at some point he may not still be around. The addiction had a strong hold on him and wasn't letting go. He knew it but was helpless to stop it.

This was not what I wanted to deal with at the time. Is this what God wanted me to find? Was this part of his plan? Just as I had accepted that Rob was gone and never walking through the front door again, now I had to deal with this new discovery. Either he knew he was going to die or he actually wanted to die. He was sick and tired of being sick and tired. He knew he had messed up with the DWI he had gotten six days prior on New Year's Eve. He had let me and himself down with his carelessness. He also knew that he was hooked on heroin and it would be almost impossible to break that deadly grip. I didn't know how to deal with the idea that my beautiful son Rob thought things were so bad that the only way out was to kill himself. He mentioned in his note that he was sick and tired of the haters. "Fuck all the fish" he said in the note.

Fish stood for "fucking ignorant shitheads," which is how he referred to people who had given him a hard time for one reason or another.

My mind started swirling with all kinds of thoughts. I was overwhelmed and couldn't control my emotions. I was filled with so many questions and doubts. I immediately thought of how I had told him that if I couldn't trust him not to take my truck, then I wasn't so sure I wanted him around. I just meant I might not want him to be living with me, of course not that I wanted him to be gone forever. Could the effect of the heroin have made him misunderstand what I meant? He knew I loved him. And I thought he loved me. I remember we talked about how the majority of suicides took place during the winter months when everything was dormant, and the snow was dirtied with cinders and grime curled up along the sides of the roads. I remember I told Rob to look for signs after I died because I would do everything I could to reach out from the "other side" and try to communicate with him. We talked about death and dying because we had that type of relationship. No topic was off-limits.

Once, I had gotten sick while working a job with Rob. I was coughing up blood. It was probably just from the dust I was breathing in while applying hydraulic cement to a house foundation wall, but it was still scary. I remember Rob seemed pretty moved by the sight of his dad taken ill and he insisted on me getting checked out. He took the lead and looked out for me just the way I would do for him. I was proud of how he handled himself and I think it brought us closer together, it tested us.

All of a sudden, I got a chill up my spine. It felt like Rob was there by my side with his hand in mine like after the paramedics had pronounced him gone. That had taken place two years and two months ago. This was now April 7, 2016, and there I was, sick to my stomach from crying and weeping to the point where I had trouble catching my breath. Discovering this note was just too much. I grabbed it and drove up to Roger's place. I parked my truck, left the driver-side door open, and ran into his house. I normally would knock, but this time I just went in and called out to Roger, who was doing some paperwork at his desk.

"I think he killed himself, Roger. I found this note and it sounds like Rob committed suicide." I handed the large manila folder to Roger and he read it.

"You know he just wasn't thinking straight, Moss. Those drugs just took over. Life's a rough road sometimes, Moss. There's not always an explanation. You can't get caught up with this note."

Well, it was too late for that. I already had. It had consumed me and I just didn't want to do anything. At that moment as I stood there, I felt I wanted to be with Rob wherever he was, Hell, Heaven, didn't matter, I wanted to be with him. It felt like he needed me. I wanted to be dead just like him. I wouldn't ever intentionally take my life, but at that moment I did pray to God to take me and let me be with Rob, with my son.

There was no rational explanation for my thoughts. They were genuine, that's all I knew. I wasn't embarrassed to express my feelings and would talk openly as I do to this day about how I don't care if I live or die. I really don't care. The only thing that gets me to work is I owe people money and have a responsibility to pay my debts. Nothing else gave me purpose to wake up in the morning like my son did. Nothing else mattered anymore.

Roger told me he was starved and ordered me to give him a ride to our favorite restaurant, the Blue Dolphin over in Apalachin. He bought me dinner and we talked about the time I was working for him when he developed the property this restaurant now sat on. I started listing all the projects Roger's company had developed. Although Roger did so much for the growth of the area, he received very little recognition whatsoever. He made Apalachin history when he sold three acres directly off exit 66 for $450,000. There were no buildings on that property, just workable land.

After dinner I drove Roger back to his hilltop home in Little Meadows, Pennsylvania, and went home myself. He called me later and talked to me for an hour or so. He knew I was in a fragile state and was checking up on me. Of course, he didn't put it like that. He just talked to me and kept me distracted, just the way he had at dinner. He knew I needed to get Rob out of my head and to focus on other things. That grief just had such a hold on me, it was almost as powerful as that heroin must have been for Rob. If ever there was a time when I needed a friend, it was then, and Roger didn't let me down. Although he would never offer anything he didn't believe in, and many times his brutal truth didn't feel like it helped at all, it was his friendship at that moment that may have saved me from my own grief.

Because of my recent discovery, I basically went through the motions with those New York rallies. Things were changing a bit because Trump started using airplane hangars to house all of the supporters. It was convenient for him and his security detail because he didn't have to go far from his 767 and the hangars held thousands of supporters at once. I didn't tell any of the rally people that I met about the horrible discovery I had made. I kept that to myself and entertained the crowds as usual.

The memories of my son managed to mess up all of my holidays. Now, instead of thinking about traditional celebrations, all of my calculations revolved around his death. Rob passed away on January 6, 2014, just seven days short of my January 13 birthday. To this day, I talk to the box that holds Rob's ashes, "Man, Rob, if you were trying to get the ole man, boy you really got to me this time!" It's true. For me, holidays no longer hold special meanings as they once did. I focus on my son's birthday and the day he died. The rest of the calendar is meaningless.

On April 23, 2016, I was at the Rider Jet Center in Hagerstown, Maryland. Thousands of supporters stood in line for the Sunday rally. There were vendors all over the place adding to the circus-like atmosphere. As the doors opened at 1:00, it became clear that thousands were going to be turned away without getting a chance to see Mr. Trump. This was the first rally where I had brought a battery-powered amplifier. My guitar and microphone were both plugged into the six-hundred-watt portable unit. I gave it a test and it was very loud, which made it so much easier to sing to the large crowds. I didn't have to go up and down the line so much. I also had "Donald Trump for President" CDs for sale. My original songs—"Trump Train," "Gonna Build a Wall," "Cherished Memories"—were all on there. I sold them for $10 each. People seemed especially interested in the ever-present red ball caps, but I sold about fifty CDs, which I thought was pretty good for my first time out as a vendor. However, selling merchandise took away from my socializing and didn't allow me to talk to folks the way I liked.

I met a couple that was selling T-shirts. One of them said, "We hate Trump and everything he stands for, but the sales are so good at his rallies we just have to go to them." I was taken aback, but upon further research found out that most of the vendors didn't care for Trump for the same reasons. It seemed confusing to me because I couldn't imagine profiting off something or someone that I didn't support. I just wouldn't operate that way, but to each his own, I guess.

It didn't take long before I met a couple that told me they had lost their daughter the year before to heroin. "She was nineteen and had hoped to become a model someday," the woman said as she showed me a photo of her daughter.

"Her name was Nicole and she was our pride and joy," the father added. The three of us talked about how somebody needs to do something about these drugs that are flooding our streets and killing our children. I realized these folks were just like me. They were trying to do anything to make life a little better for others. By voting Trump into office, we all thought that we at least would have the peace of mind that we had done something. Things weren't happening with the current administration in office and a change might be needed. For us, it was worth taking that chance.

My amplifier did have another benefit. It helped to drown out the chants from the two hundred or so protesters that lined the walkway where the attendees were waiting to enter the building. The amplifier was working so well that a Secret Service guy came over to me and asked if I could announce some basic rules about what can and cannot be taken into the rally. I knew flags were not allowed in and the vendors did as well, but they continued to sell the little Trump souvenirs for $5, only to have the security personnel take them from the supporters as they entered the building.

The next day was another Pennsylvania rally, this time at West Chester University. The university was tucked away along city streets so it was easy for protesters to get up close and personal with the supporters standing in line. As I talked about Rob while holding his picture up, I noticed the attention I was getting from different groups of kids. As I spoke of the dangers of heroin use, I saw one girl nudge her friend and another tap his friend's foot with his toe as I explained how Rob was just experimenting with heroin because his girlfriend and a few other of his friends were using the drug. I told them I had found out that someone first sprinkled some heroin in a joint they rolled and shared with my son. Apparently, that helped to get him hooked on the stuff. It was after that he started heating up the heroin on tin foil and inhaling the fumes to get a better high. He also snorted it, his friends told me, and only shortly before he died, he had started injecting the toxic mix of heroin and fentanyl into his veins. A junkie, my son was a junkie and I didn't even know it. It still amazed me that I couldn't see it. The kids were genuinely interested and asked questions about Rob and what he was like. My eyes gleamed as I told them what an ambitious, industrious guy he was before the drugs took over and changed him.

At that rally, a guy volunteered to sell my CDs for me while I was playing. Between the two of us, we sold about one hundred. That was $1,000 and it sure came in handy. Traveling to these places was getting expensive. I had already sold my backhoe, job trailer, equipment trailer, camper, and tools like welders, drill presses, and torch sets to fund my expedition. I also sold an excavator and a small dump truck. My only real regret was when I sold my trusty, money-making backhoe. All the other things I could live without, but the backhoe could come in handy when I needed to find work.

The rally in Wilkes-Barre was held at the Mohegan Sun Arena–Casey Plaza. I wasn't allowed to sell CDs on the premises. All vendors were banned from conducting business there. Word had it that this was an order that came from Trump himself. He was starting to get annoyed that people were making money on his name without his permission. I ended up giving my CDs away as I sang and shared Rob's story. Many people came up to me and told their story of loss. It seemed like an average of one in every ten people I talked to had someone in their family or knew someone who had lost a loved one to heroin or opiates of some kind. What a lot of people didn't initially understand was that opiates are the same as heroin, just a legal version of the addictive drug. Because of that, there was often an economic divide. The wealthier people were addicted to prescription opioids while folks without a lot of money often got hooked on street drugs like heroin. The common ground is that addiction knows no economic boundaries. Everyone is vulnerable.

It felt like I was telling the same story over and over, like I was on repeat. Yet I wasn't tired of doing it because each time was different. There were new people to reach at each rally. I educated people about the dangers of the drug, but also about what a really good man my son had turned out to be and how he hadn't deserved to die. I talked about how the EMTs didn't have the Narcan, a prescription drug known as the opioid antidote, and how it felt to me like my little town of Owego had basically stuck their collective heads in the sand and pretended there wasn't a heroin problem in our own backyard.

I never once mentioned the suicide note I had found on Rob's birthday. I tried hard not to even think about it. I especially didn't want to share that with the news people because then it would be everywhere. I just couldn't handle that yet. I was still trying to process it and understand exactly what had happened. Was it an accidental overdose? It was definitely an accident that he died, but he had intentionally shot three bags of heroin into his system. What did he think would happen? Was he even thinking rationally?

Probably not, but he had taken the time to write a will. It was hard to put myself in his place because I was thinking clearly, and my mind wasn't muddled up by that horrible drug. If he had actually planned it, that was something I wasn't ready to accept.

Handing out my CDs was like therapy for me. Since I was now giving them away for free, I focused on people who told me they were in the military or had previously served. It got to the point where if they said one of their relatives had been in the service, whether they were still alive or not, I gave them a CD. Sharing my story, talking about Rob, and giving away my music brought me more satisfaction than I initially realized. I started to understand that talking to people was my way of processing everything that had happened. Hearing their feedback and learning more about them just validated that I was doing right by Rob and I was helping myself heal in the process.

Still fighting back the disturbing thoughts of what Rob may have done during the final hours of his life, I decided to stick with what was working, and that was attending rallies. So I set out for Indiana. A bunch of events were being held there just ahead of their primary voting. Cruz was favored by about 12 percent over Trump according to various media predictions. Indiana was right up Trump's ally as far as his stance on keeping jobs in America because the Carrier company was located there and had announced plans to move some 1,300 jobs from Indiana to Mexico, where they were setting up shop to manufacture their air conditioner units.

The first rally I attended in that state was on April 20 in Indianapolis. The date stuck out at me as Rob often joked about 420. I was clueless to what he was talking about and he finally filled me in and said that 420 is a reference to smoking pot. There are several different stories about where it came from, and Rob said that 4:20 in the afternoon is considered the ideal time for the majority of pot smokers to light up joints and bongs. I guess it started as a college thing, but quickly the term caught on. Anything related to the number 420 was significant to pot smokers, Rob told me.

This rally was to be held at the Indiana State Fairgrounds, which to me seemed like the perfect backdrop for Trump's middle-America message. The Trump campaign rented the entire fairground property. There were no protesters nearby and absolutely no vendors allowed on the grounds as well. I brought my CDs with me and did the same as last time, giving them out to those with a connection to military service. Once in a while, I gave them to the older folks. There was a separate entrance for different groups, especially the disabled. I just wandered over to them, sang them some songs, and passed out my CDs.

Making the CD was a little difficult financially. I had sold my John Deere SG310 4×4 backhoe for $20,000, which was about $5,000 short of its actual value. When you want money fast, you tend to just get what you can at a fire sale. Most of the CD expense was for studio time. It had cost me about $10,000 when it was all said and done. I had a difficult time finding a quality studio to record all of my Trump songs: "Trump Train," "Gonna Build a Wall," "Donald Trump for President," and a bunch more. Most of the studios had recording time available, but believe it or not, when they found out what the subject matter was, they quickly said they were not interested in spending sixteen hours a day listening to songs promoting a person they absolutely despised.

After a grueling search from Newburg, New York, through Binghamton and north to Ithaca, I finally found one studio, and when I say one, I mean one. That was the only one that would take my business and record my music for me. They were a small recording studio set up in the basement of a home. It was real basic, nothing fancy, but when I listened to some of their projects, the sound quality was exactly what I wanted for my songs. I also own the copyright to the song lyrics of "Let's Make America Great Again." That might be a contributing factor as to why I got the cold shoulder from Trump after the CD came out.

Because it had been so successful, I continued using my portable amplifier. I had tested it at three rallies and it worked great. Not only could I be heard by more people, but it also saved my vocals. To mix things up, I had the CD copied to a thumb drive and then I played it through the amp and I would sing along, but the crowds seemed to like my genuine live performances better. I even had to turn down the volume on this six-hundred-watt amp because it was just so loud.

The souvenir flag issue continued, and I found it amusing. The vendors knew good and well that flags were not allowed inside, but of course they didn't tell the attendees that. They sold thousands of those to unknowing supporters. I suppose the $5 price tag was very appealing to many people. It was much cheaper than the $20 "Make America Great Again" hats or the Trump T-shirts for $30 or more. Every rally had garbage cans that were eventually overflowing with those damn Trump flags. Some would tear off the fabric part and just throw the stick away. Anyway, it was interesting to see the exact same scene play out at each rally.

Indianapolis was a turning point because it really showed everyone how upset Trump was that people were selling stuff with his name on it and neither him nor his campaign were benefitting. It would seem that the vendors in a way helped promote Trump's run for president because of the promotional aspect, but they apparently didn't see it that way. Maybe that's why he didn't really jump up and down with joy when I produced a CD complete with music about him and his run for president.

The Evansville rally was scheduled for April 28, and since I was nearby again, I dropped in on Brandy and her family in Dayton. Brandy made it a priority to tell me that she was a Bernie Sanders girl all the way. I told her that was fine to have our own beliefs. She was just graduating from nursing school and invited me to stay with them for the week. I ate the healthiest meals while visiting that household. I could feel the presence of love the minute I walked into their home. The kids greeted me politely and Brandy hugged me, saying that I must be starved from my journey. Her husband, Seth, who at the time was five years into serving our country in the air force, asked me if I wanted to go to the store with him while he picked up some building materials for a project he was working on. He called out to Brandy, "Hey, Babe, I've got to run to Lowe's real quick. Do you need anything while I'm out?"

"Oh, bring back a million dollars, that would be nice," Brandy replied jokingly while she entered the kitchen. Brandy was a health nut for sure and the evidence was all around—fruits, vegetables, fish, chicken, you name it. I'd never guess it from looking at her, but she had a sweet tooth. "Could you stop by a bakery in one of those super-duper markets and pick up some kind of raspberry-filled muffins?"

It was just so nice seeing a happy, functional family unit, especially after what I had experienced growing up and in my own adulthood. I watched from the sidelines as the kids played together and joked around with each other. I'm not saying things were perfect, but it was clear that there was an emphasis on family and togetherness. It just warmed my heart to see such genuine love and respect for each other. This was the kind of family I had always wanted to provide for Rob, but I just hadn't been able to get it right.

Brandy's mom was my third wife and had been my girlfriend from fifth grade through high school. I wasn't interested at first due to the harassment from my friends, but once she got her braces off, I thought she was hot. I asked her to a dance. At first, she said, "You never liked me before, but now I'm looking good to you?" She eventually gave in and we were one. In sixth grade, she would put apples in my locker and bring me baked goods that she had made at home. I really thought we would marry and have a nice family. We were both in choir and I'll always remember how beautiful she looked in her pink and blue dresses. We talked about how many children we would have one day. I used to visit her when she was babysitting a family with five kids. One of the kids dumped a bowl of popcorn over my head. She said, "You better get used to it because one day we will have kids of our own."

I messed that up because I worked on my motocross bike and prepared for a big national race rather than taking her to the prom. She dated some goofball, but ended up with an upperclassman who had a real nice, lifted pickup. In 1977 that was a big deal, at least where we grew up. On prom night a friend of mine called me from a grocery store pay phone and told me that my "old lady" was with a guy named Chuck, the one with the pickup. I went to the party and confronted her and hot rod Chuck. He was a pretty good size, and I really didn't want to tangle with him. I asked her what she was doing, and she said, "You said you didn't have time to take me to the prom, so I found someone who did."

I was so mad. And hurt. But I realized that I had brought the hurt upon myself. I just never thought she would throw away what we had just like that. But then again, all I had to do was take her to the prom. A couple of years after the prom incident, I ran into her again and we reconnected, igniting our romance. That was the first time we slept together. During our earlier dating, we were much more innocent, just kissing, holding hands, and talking about how when we got married we would have a big family and live out in the country.

It wasn't until 2003 that we actually did get married to each other, and that was after she had been married once and I had taken the plunge twice. We tried to connect like we had in the past and for a long time we made it work, living out our childhood dream of just being together and loving each other. We talked and laughed and somehow, once again, I messed that up and it was a similar situation. I once again got caught up in work and other things and got tired of the glass always being half empty. One day I sounded off and said, "Why don't you go find someone to sleep with, fall in love, and get the hell out of my life? I mean it! Just go find someone that will love you for the next thirty years and get out, and take your carpet-peeing, piece-of-shit dogs with you. Don't forget your crying, spoiled baby daughter either."

Three months later, I came home from work, expecting dinner on the table, and there in front of my home in Owego, New York, was a moving van and a couple pickup trucks. My wife was walking out the front door with her suitcase and a big shit-eating grin on her face. I'm sure she timed her departure so that I would witness her dramatic exit. I said, "What the hell is going on here and where are you headed to with your suitcase and what are these trucks doing here?"

She came up to me, standing practically nose to nose, with her pretty little blonde head and sparkly blue eyes. Then she said in a whisper with a confidence and cockiness that I hadn't seen before, "Be careful what you wish for, asshole." With that, she turned and walked swiftly to the passenger door of one of the pickup trucks, got in, and flipped me off as she drove away. Unfortunately, this seemed to be a scene that played out in front of me several times in my life.

I had my son living with me then and he was devastated that our family was splitting up. He had enjoyed having a stepmother and sister and this had hit him pretty hard. For the first time, he piped up when I started laying blame on everyone but myself. "Really, Pop? Do you really think it's everyone else that's the cause of your breakups? Don't you think maybe, just maybe, it might be you?"

That's when I realized just how important this family life had been to him. He was right, of course, that I was placing blame everywhere without taking any responsibility. I don't know how or why, but I just kept creating an atmosphere of anger and hostility in my home life. No matter how good things were, I managed to screw it up. I didn't take it as seriously as I should have. This time it was affecting the most important person in my life, my son Rob. With my wife gone, he and I had started to argue and fight frequently. I felt like my whole life was falling apart and I didn't know how to stop it. It was a difficult time for all of us.

When Brandy opened up her home to me, without any prejudice or judgment, I was so happy. Not only that, I was truly grateful because she didn't have to do that. I hadn't been the best stepfather I could have been, but to her credit, she realized that we had both grown and changed over the years. We did talk about some of the good times we shared as a family, and I was truly proud of the woman she had become.

Over twelve thousand people attended the rally at the Old National Events Plaza that started at noon. This was where Trump announced that Governor Mike Pence would be his running mate. He went through his normal media bashing, calling them "scum" and "lowlifes." He talked about border control and how Mexico was going to pay for the wall. He also cursed Carrier and said all jobs that were slated to go to Mexico would be brought back to Indiana. Then he promised if he became president that ISIS would be no more. He would also present a healthcare bill that would be "one hundred times better" than Obamacare, to fight the opioid crisis. There were also some other general things he promised to the crowd—no more NAFTA, no more corruption, going to make America great again, and on and on. I thought to myself, *It will be interesting to see how many statements actually come true.*

The Fort Conrad, Indiana, rally was on May 1 at the Allen County War Memorial Coliseum. I went to a local gun show between these rallies and rented a booth. I sat there selling a few CDs and talking about Trump, but it didn't set the world on fire and I barely made back the money it cost me for the table and chair. I did find a guy who sold me USA hats for about $3 each. I bought a bunch of them from him and later sold them at rallies for $10 and included my CD. That helped me make a few dollars and I realized that if I had tried, I could have sold hats and really made money off of these rallies, but that wasn't my intention.

I wanted to stick to my mission of talking about my wonderful son and the dangers of heroin use. I continued to keep my recent discovery of Rob's suicide note to myself. Believe me, after reading that note, I had a lot to say to Rob's box as he rode beside me in the front seat of my pickup. "Oh Rob, if you were trying to get the ole man back for something, you got me good, son. You got me good." On many of those drives, the grief would sometimes just take hold of me without warning. I would find myself driving down the road and crying uncontrollably. I couldn't slow down my thoughts as they swirled around inside my head. I would replay the arguments we had, wondering which one had made such a devastating impact on him. I thought of the girl on heroin who told me that I hadn't shown my son enough love and I didn't understand him. She didn't even know me or Rob, but maybe she had a point. Maybe I didn't really know what was going on inside his head and what he thought about the things I had put him through. The divorces and breakups might have just been too much for him to take. I realized that these late-night "what if" sessions were not healthy or productive. There was no way to know exactly what was going on with him, but it was hard not to wonder. The lonesome highways made it even more difficult to push those thoughts away.

I headed off to South Bend, Indiana, for a rally at the Century Center. Supporters and protesters showed up starting at noon and the event wouldn't start until 7:00 that evening. A few scuffles broke out between the supporters and protesters, but nothing too violent. I noticed more and more young men with shaved heads at the Indiana rallies. Many of them wore hats and clothing with the Confederate flag prominently displayed. It seemed like the popularity of these events was giving other groups of people reason to show up and make their voices heard. They knew it would be well reported on national and international media outlets. This rally was very similar to the last one. Trump didn't even change his message. He basically made the same promises to his supporters about everything and told them that if he won their state of Indiana, his opponents, Cruz and Kasich, would be done for good. This was one thing that he was exactly right about. Trump won Indiana and it was all over for his opponents. Everyone eventually dropped out of the race and he went on unchallenged. I planned on going to the Northwest to visit Washington, Oregon, and other places, but then the rallies stopped for a while. I think Trump went to some big shot meeting or maybe did some planning with his campaign. Whatever the case, the rallies stopped. Maybe that was because, finally, Donald J. Trump was the undisputed winner of the Republican Party presidential candidacy.

I checked the Trump for President website daily in search of the upcoming rallies. Those events had become so popular that they could post it online for the next day and it would be packed. I couldn't imagine all of the last-minute travel arrangements being made and the TV networks scurrying to get plane tickets for their reporters. Also, there were thousands of people taking off work and making plans to be at the next rally to support their candidate. It was truly mind-boggling. Another reason for the short notices was to discourage organized protesters from getting some kind of disruption planned in advance. I'm sure it was much more difficult to mobilize a lot of people and arrange travel on one day's notice. No matter how short the notice, all the major news outlets made sure to get there with their ever-present cameras and news trucks parked as close to the rally as possible, vying for access to the action.

I received a call from my newfound friends Larry and Char, the couple who gave us a place to stay during the month of January at their farm in Iowa. They extended an invitation to me to come and stay with them for a while. With no rallies planned, my schedule was wide open and I accepted their invitation and headed to Ottumwa. It wasn't a long journey, only 375 miles. By this time, I was used to twelve-hour driving trips. This one was easy. I took my time getting there, arriving at the beautiful farm at 7:00 in the evening. I wasn't thinking about dinner since I was a few hours later than I had expected to be, but they had kept a warm plate of food in the oven covered with tin foil just for me. Meeting people like that helped to reaffirm my faith in our country.

Although they were not Mormon, these folks had been on the Oregon Trail and reenacted the journey of the early Mormons. They didn't drive fancy new cars, but they seemed to be doing well out on that farm. I could tell by the presence of their equipment like tractors, bulldozers, and scraper pans used to maintain their three-hundred-acre spread. In addition, they were taking on another project—building a new house on their land. It was about four thousand square feet and all the wood, cabinets, and carpentry was custom. They owned several other homes in the area that they either rented out or were carrying the mortgage for this person or the other who was down on their luck. I rode around with Larry and visited some of his friends. I even attended a birthday party for one of their grandchildren in a nearby town. I was treated and accepted as one of the family. It felt so good to have these folks, who could have been my parents, tell me they loved me like their own. In exchange for their hospitality, I pitched in by helping to fix a tractor, mend fences, and work in the garage on various projects that were in progress.

I guess the one thing that I remember the most about my visit to their farm was going to church with them. It was a cowboy church held at the local fairgrounds. Larry would bring a huge wooden cross and some other props like a pulpit and some milk cans. The cans were set up for donations. There wasn't likely a lot of money among the attendees. They were a small crowd of about forty regular working-class folks. What they may have lacked in material possessions they certainly made up for in fellowship and neighborly love. It was amazing to watch these folks as they brought a carefully prepared dish from their own kitchen to share with the others after services. The church service we attended was held on Saturday night so that everyone could go to their regular church the next morning. They encouraged me to participate and I sang five of my Christian songs. It was so wonderful meeting all the nice folks who attended. A week later, they took me to another cowboy church in a different town that followed a similar format. Like before, I spoke a little and sang some of my songs. The preacher man whispered in my ear as I left the stage, "And you said you couldn't preach."

Earlier, he had asked me if I wanted to do some preaching along with my singing and I said, "I'm no preacher." But maybe I was because once I was onstage, I did speak the words that came to me. What I said up there was real simple: "Being a Christian is kind of like riding a bull in competition. After you ride for eight seconds, you get scored on your ride. Even if your score is not that good, no one can ever take that ride away from you. Same for being a Christian. Once you accept Jesus Christ as your personal Savior, no one can take that away. Your score may not be the highest, but whatever it is, it's yours and no one can deny that."

I had pointed to a man at the service with his wife and three children who were restless in their seats. "You, sir, in the back. What's your name if I may ask?"

He said quietly, "It's Jim."

I said, "Okay, Jim, let's say you stopped by your friend's house after work to help him load his lawn mower on a trailer or whatever, so you're helping him, and he looks at you and says 'hey, did I see your truck at church Sunday morning' in a joking manner. The wrong answer from you, Jim, would be, 'oh yeah, well I went there for the wife and kids.' The best answer would be, 'Well yes, I was there, praise the Lord I say. Hey, we got a men's Bible study on Wednesday nights. Maybe you'd like to stop by. Lots of cake and coffee.' What I'm saying here, Jim, is you can't be ashamed of your beliefs. You have to wear the cloak of God proudly. How many times have you asked someone if they were a Christian and they responded, 'Well yeah I believe in God'? Your response should be, 'Well, Satan believed in God. He didn't worship him, but he believed he was real. Believing is not enough. If you're flying in a small plane and it develops engine problems, believing that parachute will float you safely to the ground is not enough. You have to put it on and wear it.'"

That's what I said while I was on stage and then I launched into my song. I didn't really think of it as preaching. I was just sharing how I felt. After the preacher man finished his sermon, he told the congregation that I didn't ask for any money whatsoever, but if they felt moved by what I had said they could give me a "big ole hallelujah handshake." Afterward, when we were eating, all these people came up and shook my hand. Each and every time, I felt something clasped in the palm and ended the night with a good collection of folded bills and personal checks. I guess I had a look of surprise on my face because a kid about ten years old appeared by my side, his lips smeared with chocolate icing from the cake in his hand. He said, "That's what we call a hallelujah handshake, Mr. Moss." When I got back to the farm with a full heart and stomach, I counted $375. My hosts told me I should start preaching, that I had a real gift for touching people's soul. I responded the same as I did to the preacher man, "I'm no preacher, I'm just me."

Three weeks went by without a single rally schedule on the website. I was getting a little antsy since I had basically put everything else on hold. I couldn't really start up a job and then stop for another rally. I had to see this through and finish my mission and my tribute to my son. I had promised myself that I would honor him as long as I could, and I would never go back on my word to him. Just as I started to really worry, I was checking the website when a rally popped up for Albuquerque, New Mexico. I was excited! Finally, we were back in business. This one was going to be at the convention center on May 24. That would be a little bit of a drive and I needed to get to it. I was still at the farm with my friends. I packed up my freshly laundered clothes and said good-bye to those generous folks. Before I left, they made me a proposition. They said they would love to have me live with them and join them in serving the Lord at the cowboy churches around the country. They had plans of building a big Christian camp and inviting congregations from cowboy churches around the United States to attend a yearly jamboree of sorts.

I told them how grateful I was for the offer. I said, "You never know, but I'm not homeless. I have my own place, but I would be honored to come here and serve the Lord with you folks." Who knows? Maybe someday I'll end up staying there. If I had learned anything in these past couple of years, it was that I needed to make the most of my time on earth. It was my responsibility and my honor to share Rob's story and message. Right now, the best way to do that was by attending these rallies. I had already garnered plenty of media attention and countless interviews. That's not counting the hundreds, if not thousands, of people I'd sung and talked to. Now wasn't the time, but maybe later a cowboy church would be a good place for me to continue my work. I decided to leave it in God's hands and focus on the rally in front of me. I got in my truck and drove away. I felt sad as I watched the sweet couple get smaller and smaller in my rearview mirror. I wiped a tear from my eye, pointed my Dodge Ram pickup in the direction of Albuquerque, and never looked back.

I arrived at the Albuquerque Convention Center on May 23, a day before the rally. I always liked to arrive as early as possible, and a full day before was a real luxury. That would give me time to get my bearings, scope out the facility, and determine the best place to park my trusty pickup with Trump signs and bumper stickers generously displayed. Many times, when my funds were running low, I would pay $5 and pull into a parking garage. Then I would have a protected place to catch up on my sleep. The only problem was that I usually couldn't get good cell or internet service on my phone in the concrete garages. The web on my phone was where I kept up with the daily events, kept in touch with the world (outside of Trump), and watched a movie or two sometimes.

When I got to the rally, I knew things were going to be a little different. I don't know why, but I just had this feeling. Things felt . . . heightened. Maybe it was because there had been a dearth of events for so long. The Trump supporters were definitely in the thousands. This was apparently true Trump territory; there was no question about that. The crowd was also much more diverse than others I had seen. Many different ethnic groups were well represented. The convention center was located in the downtown area. It wasn't as protected as the rented fairgrounds or airplane hangars. That meant the protesters were allowed to be up close and personal with the supporters, their adversaries. This time, the protesters were very aggressive. They were even swearing at me as I played my Trump songs and did my mini-speeches supporting Trump. I would call people up to my microphone and have them say their name and where they were from in exchange for a "Donald Trump for President" CD. The protesters were about three hundred strong and were being held back by seventy-five police officers in full riot gear including batons and helmets with face shields. The presence of the no-nonsense officers seemed to keep any real violence at bay, and I was thankful for that. That morning, I had noticed three huge buses sitting in an abandoned factory parking lot about four blocks away from the convention center. I figured they were for the paid protesters, but I wasn't sure. I just knew that when I saw buses that meant word was spreading and people were attending in huge numbers.

My theory soon proved correct when I looked up from another of my songs to see that the throng of protesters had at least doubled. They were heckling and yelling as loud as they could while I was singing a Trump song on my Martin guitar adorned with Trump stickers. I'm not sure what came over me. I am generally a peaceful person, at least these days, but all the taunting and name-calling just got to me. I realized I had thousands of supporters and the police were there "to serve and protect." I felt kind of secure and safe. I fell back to my mischievous ways and dreamed up a plan to get back at all these protesters.

Up until that day, I had purposely avoided playing one of the songs I had written called "Gonna Build a Wall" with some of the lyrics including "and make Mexico pay for it all." It was controversial and divisive when Trump first talked about it. I was trying not to anger anyone. I wanted to spread my message positively. I didn't want to piss off people. However, this seemed like a different situation. I cued up my thumb drive to that song and planned my exit as I knew I would have to leave as soon as it was done. I pointed my portable PA system at the protesters and called into the microphone. "Here's a song for all of you protesters to let you know we're going to build a wall, and if you're from Mexico, well, you're going to pay for it, plain and simple." The officers glanced over their shoulders at me. There wasn't anything they could do. I had the freedom of speech on my side, the same as those name-calling protesters.

"Your son was a junkie, man, and it's nobody's fault but yours," one man yelled out.

"The Trump Troubadour is a loser," another one chimed in.

I had taken about as much as I was going to take. I pushed the play button and the song cranked up. The words "gonna build a wall" were bouncing and echoing off the surrounding buildings. It was twice as loud as normal due to the acoustics. I saw that the crowd was visibly upset, even pushing into the riot police as they became more uneasy. I grabbed my stuff and started walking down the sidewalk away from the protesters. I asked an officer if he could walk with me to my truck. He told me to turn that song off and leave. "What were you thinking?" he asked me. I told him they were calling me names and yelling shit about my dead son. The officer led me across the street, and when I got to the parking lot, we both heard a commotion and turned around to look back at the crowd. In an instant, things had changed and there was a full-blown riot. The actual rally had ended, and the protesters had pushed through the blockade and turned over vendor tables, set T-shirts on fire, and even picked up one of the vendor tables and heaved it through the front door of the convention center. It was totally out of control and I wasted no time in getting the hell out of there. I smiled the same way I had when I was a kid playing with the matches my mom used to light her cigarette. Not sure what got into me, but Christianity went right out the window and Satan had entered my body. I just hoped no one got hurt. The media wasted no time in reporting about the Trump riot in Albuquerque, New Mexico. It only added fuel to the anti-Trump rhetoric that swirled around the news and social media.

There was a notice on Trump's website for a rally the next day in Anaheim, California. It was scheduled for May 25 at 12:30 p.m. I had left the Albuquerque circus atmosphere at 5:00 p.m. and it was about eight hundred miles to Anaheim, which would take about sixteen hours with fuel stops. I took a nap at a rest area and arrived at the convention center about 10:00 a.m. I left my amp in the truck this time and only took my guitar because all the supporters were gathered in a large waiting room. Surprisingly, they allowed me in the building with my guitar. I had a sack of CDs and managed to sell a few here and there until they told me I could not sell any more. I could give them away, but no sales. I played guitar and the ones who wanted a CD would sneak me some money.

I was very tired at this point, but was happy I had made it there. A supporter with a bullhorn outside yelled at the protesters and told them to go back to Mexico where they belonged. At least I hadn't gone *that* far back in Albuquerque. Anyway, the weather was beautiful, and I was feeling good about being in California. It gave me a renewed sense of purpose. If I had known beforehand that there would be a bunch of rallies in California, I probably wouldn't have headed to Billings, Montana, so hastily, but since I was driving solo, I had to manage my time carefully.

The Montana rally was held at the Rim Rock Auto Arena and ten thousand people were expected to show up to support Trump. Then I saw that Trump was speaking at the Petroleum Conference in Bismarck, North Dakota, the next day. This was getting to be too much. I just couldn't keep up with that 767 Trump flew around in! I decided to make some tough decisions. I scratched the Bismarck appearance, which turned out to be a smart move since I found out that there was only a small handful of supporters in attendance.

The one in Billings was very cool. There were lots of vendors and friends that I hadn't seen in a while. The protesters were confined to a small corner of the parking lot at the far outer perimeter of the facility. Those were the best situations for a successful rally because that meant there would be very few problems with protesters. I drove about 1,200 miles in one day to get there before the start time and I was just exhausted. After I made my appearance, I met with many folks who said meth was a bigger problem in that area than heroin. We all agreed that addiction was a true epidemic, regardless of which horrible drug led to it.

Next, I headed to Fresno, a town where I used to live. The rally was at the Selland Arena on May 27 at 10:00 in the morning. This was not one of my best decisions. First, I was extremely tired from driving and I still hadn't slept much since New Mexico. Once I arrived, it was obvious that there were many more protesters than some of the other rallies, and while some of the others may have been compensated monetarily, these people were definitely there of their own volition. They seemed to have a score to settle. I didn't have a good feeling about it. I parked my pickup on the street about five blocks away from the arena. I left the amp in the truck and I played for the diehard supporters already in line at 6:00 a.m. to see their candidate in person. When I returned to my truck, I couldn't believe it. The driver's side window was smashed in and someone had stolen my d/c converter and digital camera. I had hidden the camera from sight by shoving it under some clothes on the floor, but once the window was broken, they were able to find it. The camera was replaceable, but the memory card that was attached held all of the photos I had taken during my journey. Fortunately, I had uploaded some to Facebook along the way, but the majority were on that card. I felt sick. The only good thing about being in Fresno was that I visited some distant relatives and reconnected. Otherwise, it was a horrible experience.

I was off to Sacramento, California, to the Jet Center at the airport for a May 29 rally. I played guitar and did some interviews as I had at other rallies with this news station or the other. Protesters were present but not a threat in any way. Peace and love was the message they brought to the rally that day.

The next few events were in California, and the violence level varied depending on the location, although none were as bad as Fresno. The one in San Jose on June 2 drew a huge crowd, about five thousand supporters. However, it looked like almost the same number of protesters had made their way to the rally. At one point, the protesters burned Trump shirts and hats that they had stolen from vendors. Then they jumped on a police car and threw eggs at supporters and cops. I didn't play there or talk about my son. I had learned to assess the situation first and then decide if it seemed like a peaceful venue or not. This time, I quietly slipped away and did not bring attention to myself. San Jose was a bad scene and I began to realize the kind of violence that was to be expected in towns with large populations of immigrants.

I headed to the Redding Municipal Airport for the rally on June 3. It was the first outdoor rally since the one in Boca Raton where the Secret Service struggled to manage the ultralights flying overhead. This was a very nice event and everyone was bonding over the commotion that had just taken place in San Jose and earlier in Fresno. I talked to a vendor friend of mine and he said he had lost everything he had on the table. Cops took his report, but the protesters were long gone by that point.

After Redding, I was broke and tired. I headed northeast and ended up in Montana somewhere on the original trail that Lewis and Clark blazed. I contacted a nearby cowboy church and arranged to attend services and play some of my Christian songs. I met the nice married couple who ran the church. There were not very many people who attended the service, but it was nice. They took a love offering for me and I ended up with about one hundred bucks in my pocket. I stayed an extra day in my truck since I didn't know them very well and didn't want to impose. They did take me to dinner the next day, and afterward, I headed east. I got to Bismarck and stopped at a small diner. I asked them if there was a mission or something where I might get a bite to eat and maybe a bed for the night. They didn't have anything like that, but after I explained who I was and what I was doing, they came up with the address of a bookstore that sometimes helped the needy. Many in the restaurant realized I was the guy who lost his son to heroin, referring to me as "The Trump Troubadour."

I entered the front door of the bookstore, which was literally filled with books stacked from the floor to the ceiling. Piles of books. All over. A few chairs were scattered in the corner with books piled up all around them. "Hello, I was told you folks help out people in need sometimes," I called out.

A man appeared. "Well, my girlfriend owns this store and has helped a family now and again when things got bad for them, but that's about it."

I sat and told the gray-haired, bearded man in his sixties about how I'd been following Trump around and had run out of money. When I finished with my story, which also included the recent trouble I had at the rallies in California and New Mexico, the man jumped up and said, "You can stay at my house!"

When his girlfriend returned, we visited for a short while and the gentleman asked me to follow him to his apartment. There, he pointed to the couch and told me I could bunk there. He said there was no time limit and I could move on when I was ready. I just had to make sure to return his key to the front door. He also pointed out that I had to buy my own food and could use a small area in the fridge that he began clearing out for me.

"Why are you doing this for me?" I asked. He said that he just felt he could trust me and wanted to help. He had been seeing me in the news over the past few months playing my guitar, and both he and his wife were Trump supporters. This blew my mind. I'd prayed to God I could find someplace to sleep and eat, and that's what I had found. I had a bed to sleep in and a roof over my head for as long as I needed. I had a key to the apartment of a man who I had never met before in my life. This kind of stuff just doesn't happen. Incidents on the road like that continued to restore my faith in people, especially Americans, and of course in God.

Soon I took off from North Dakota, but once again I ran out of money on the road. I made a sign that read "Will play for food or gas." When that didn't pan out, I called a trucking company that one of my friends had told me about and asked them if they could send me some money for gas and I'd come to work for them in exchange. I told them I was stranded and was on the Trump Trail. They knew who I was when I said I was the guy with the cowboy hat who had lost his son to heroin. Word had definitely gotten around. It was a small, family-owned business and they sent me money twice before I finally made it to Ohio where they were located. As agreed, I drove trucks for them and they would give me time off as needed so I could continue to attend Trump rallies. They were amazing folks and it was a blessing that they came into my life when they did. (In fact, I continue to work for Marcellus Energy. Richard and Gloria Tubbs have been so good to me.)

As summer approached, the campaign was getting more intense. It was clear that it would be a showdown between Trump and Clinton. Everyone on the campaign trail was ready and it was obvious to all of us, despite early polls to the contrary, that Donald Trump would be the next president of the United States.

There was a rally on June 9 at the coliseum in Richmond, Virginia. It was a totally different scene from past events mainly because the police departments were poised for battle after hearing about the mess out west. It became standard operating procedure for the police to put out warnings that anyone breaking the law would be arrested. Violence would not be tolerated. They didn't want a repeat of the chaos. Because of those warnings, there was no violence and nothing out of the ordinary. I did run into my vendor friend Whitey and he was still doing well, selling merchandise like crazy.

June 28 was pretty emotional for me. A rally was held at the Ohio University campus and it was mostly attended by college students. As I was talking to a group of kids and showing them a picture of Rob, I looked over and saw a young man across the lawn that looked just like my son. I mean, he had a backpack just like Rob's, his hair was the same, his build—it was alarming. I knew logically that it wasn't him, but I approached anyway. He wasn't headed to the rally, and by the time I scooted across the lawn, he was gone. I looked down the sidewalk at all the kids, scanning the crowd for any sign of the guy. I'm not sure how to explain it, but my heart had picked up its pace and my mind started spinning. Was this some sign from him that he was here? That he was okay? That was a silly thing to think, right?

I found a seat on a nearby bench and just took a minute to gather myself. What the hell was I doing? What if I had found that kid and approached him? It would have probably freaked him out. What the hell was going on? Was I losing my mind? I had those kinds of thoughts often. I would know rationally that something was impossible, but there was always a glimmer of hope that just maybe he was here somehow. Maybe I really was going crazy. I went back to my place at the rally and told the group of students what I was going through. They were all supportive and seemed understanding. I played "Cherished Memories" with more emotion than I ever had before. By the end of the song, I was in tears. I had written that about my boy and it was still very raw. It was a tough day for sure.

A month later, I was at the Huntington Center in Toledo, Ohio, for the July 27 rally. There were thousands of supporters and the mood was happy and upbeat. With Trump on a recent winning streak, his supporters were feeling more and more confident. On August 21, I went to Akron, Ohio, at the University of Akron. It was there that I concentrated on the kids. I used my microphone and PA speaker to talk to many groups that approached. As I shared my story and talked about my son, my mind wandered, and I could visualize him injecting all of that laced heroin into his veins, imagining the fentanyl taking hold of his mind, messing with his clarity. I remembered that when I found him, how he had his hands carefully folded across his chest as he went to sleep for the last time. His life, as I knew it, was over that cold day, January 6, 2014. There were so many students that I knew Rob's story would resonate with them and it did. I knew I was doing the right thing and at that moment I had reached at least those kids who were there in front of me.

The Republican National Convention (RNC) took place in Cleveland July 18–21 and it was amazing. The crowd was larger than any of the previous events. I played Donald Trump songs directly across from two hundred Muslim protesters in the city's town square. There were at least fifty cops on bicycles who rode around and monitored the situation. They had some sort of protest going on, but it was nonviolent, and I never minded those. I met a very nice grandmother who had her five-year-old grandson with her. She was African American, and her name was Sherry. She told me how her daughter, the little boy's mother, had dropped him off at her house and never returned. She and her boyfriend were drug addicts and didn't want the responsibility of a child. They probably knew that they couldn't raise him anyway, but it was still a crappy thing to do to this nice woman. She told me that she hadn't heard from them since and didn't even know if they were still alive. Nonetheless, she took it all in stride and was taking in the events at the convention. Unfortunately, this hadn't been the first time I'd heard a story like that. It was alarmingly common among addicts. They can't think clearly so they don't make good decisions.

Otherwise, there was a lot of activity at the RNC, but the violence was minimal. The headlines the next day said something like "they expected a riot and got a block party." That was true because it was a very celebratory atmosphere. The police had bought ten thousand zip-tie handcuffs and used only ten of them. I played music with a woman in a Black Lives Matter T-shirt, and by the end of the day, "Bikers for Trump" were dancing arm in arm with protesters. It's true!

I finished the Trump Trail with a few more rallies. There was one in Hershey, Pennsylvania, another in Scranton, and finally one in Manchester, New Hampshire. At that one, the Trump team called me to the front of the stage and had me stand directly in front of Mr. Trump for his entire speech. I was recognized along with some other VIPs for my support of our candidate. They even allowed me to leave, go play music for people outside, then come back in where my spot up front was waiting for me. This was the first time the Trump team really showed gratitude for what I had done all year.

It felt amazing.

7

LONELY

I often think about how I felt after getting the blood test back that indi-cated there was a 99.9 percent chance that Rob was my son. It didn't take long before I decided the best thing to do was move to California. I wanted to be a father to this child, not just someone on the other end of a phone call who sends gifts on holidays. I thought of the sacrifices my parents made with my dad living in the basement and my mom pretending everything was going to get better. I had been so excited by this surprise gift. There was no doubt in my mind that this happened for a reason, that out of this dysfunctional relationship came something wonderful—a son. After my dif-ficult upbringing, this was my chance to lead by example and do things the right way. Finding out that I was a father was the best day of my life, and then I found out that since his mother was not fit to take care of him, I could be getting custody. I was beyond excited even though I wasn't schooled in parenting. I thought for sure I could do a better job than my own parents had. It turned out that I was wrong, and like my dad always yelled at me, I guess I did "fuck up a free lunch."

When the State of California flew representatives to Alabama to take Rob from his mom and put him in a foster home until transport papers were ob-tained, I was ecstatic. When I think of it now, I feel awful. I shouldn't have done something so potentially damaging to Rob. I was only thinking about what I wanted. It was just like my selfishness during the Trump Trail when

I overlooked many issues in Trump's campaign that I disagreed with and focused only on what was important to me at the time.

When Rob was flown to California and placed once again in foster care until the temporary custody paperwork was completed, I couldn't imagine what he was going through. I'm sure he was scared and confused. I'd often lie in bed at night thinking about all of those things. I'd try to imagine myself in one of those small, uncomfortable metal beds at the foster home and wonder what Rob must have been thinking. He must have been terrified. When he was about eighteen months old and still at the California foster home, the caregiver decided she would take him for his first haircut. He had long blond hair and for some reason she took it upon herself to take him to a barber while he was in her care. I don't know if she was trying to show her control over him or exert her temporary authority, but I was not happy about that. Maybe she hadn't meant anything by it, but this was his first haircut and to me that was a big deal. I wanted to be there for all his "firsts" in life and this woman had taken one of those away from me.

Despite those challenges, I decided to focus on the positives. I not only had a son, but he ended up living with me. It was a total lifestyle change, and I was ready. To prepare, I went out west in a camper so at least I'd have a place to stay until I got situated. Fortunately, my mom agreed to move out there with me to help look after Rob. During that time, she would remind me daily how she had sacrificed the relationship with her current boyfriend to help me out. That was just the way she was. If she did you a favor, she would tell you how much you should appreciate what she was doing.

Like many parent-child relationships, the one with my mother was complex and ever-changing. While she had her flaws, she really did do her best to make sure that my sister and I had clean clothes and plenty of food. She also loved the holidays and bought Christmas presents for our aunts, uncles, cousins, and grandparents. After my father would leave the house when the two were fighting, she would say things to us like, "your father's off his rocker, he's gone cuckoo-cuckoo, cuckoo-cuckoo mongo!" She'd look at me and say, "I hope you don't grow up to be cuckoo-cuckoo." I was happy to have a good relationship with my mom. Her sister and brother were always so kind to my sister and me.

As an adult, I was fortunate to consider my mom a very good friend as well. We talked and laughed about the crazy situations I got into. They weren't funny at the time, but with reflection we bonded over them. My mom did sacrifice her relationship with her boyfriend to help me when I needed it the most. She relocated to assist me with Rob and I'm not sure how I could have done it without her. She also sent me money in times when I would fall on my face in the real world. In contrast, my dad once sent me a dollar and said "have a beer on me" when I asked him for help. "We are the manager of our own affairs," he would always say.

After I obtained custody, Rob and I bonded really well. There were three of us in tight quarters living in the camper, but we were together and that was most important. I remember walking with my boy to the campground showers and a screech owl swooped down so close we could feel the breeze he created. We would also walk around this big pond that was home to fifty or sixty geese. During mating season, we found a mother goose sitting on her eggs. The goose stuck her head out and snapped at us. Rob got scared so I tried to calm him down. "Watch this, I'll show that goose who is boss," I said. I reached out and grabbed her beak. "She can't bite us now." All of a sudden, the goose started whacking my arm with her wing. I couldn't believe how powerful she was. I had to let her go because I thought for sure she was going to break my arm. Once I pulled back, I watched as my arm swelled up and turn red. It was a dumb thing to do, but we laughed about it for years.

It was amazing to have this little person to do things with and I really did get to see the world through his eyes. It was cool to watch him experience things for the first time. Everything was so exciting to him. I tried to find interesting things to show him on a daily basis. Once I took him to the railroad tracks and placed pennies and quarters on one of the rails. Then we went on to the store. On our way back, the train had passed by so we searched the section of the track that I had marked with a tree branch. It was fun to watch him find the coins and marvel over the new shape they had taken, flatter than a pancake. These times we spent together in that park often reminded me of the idyllic scenes from *The Andy Griffith Show* that I had longed for when I was a little kid, especially the opening scene where they walked down the dirt road to go fishing. It was now my turn to do things the right way, the way I had dreamed. I knew that show was made up, but the feelings it inspired in me were very real.

To complete our little family in California, I wanted to find someone to be with, a woman who would be nurturing and caring for me and my boy. I even joined a dating service, which was a relatively new concept at the time. On their first attempt, the service matched me up with a redhead named Lisa. Her family lived nearby and was well known in the grape-growing industry, which was very big in that area. Her parents were divorced, and she didn't have a great relationship with her mother. From what she told me, she had been abused by a family member until she was eleven years old and her mother was aware but never did anything about it. Lisa had two sons. They were good boys and the four of us did a lot of things together. While Lisa stayed at home, the guys would go camping or to the NASCAR races or some other outdoor activity. Every weekend, I tried to make sure we had something fun planned.

I was glad to see that Rob took to his new family very quickly. Lisa and I got married and we were all good for each other and everyone got along surprisingly well. We had dinners together and made a lot of memories. I was just so grateful that Rob seemed to be healthy and happy. I made sure to take care of him as best I could. I took him to church, to the doctor for shots, and to the dentist. I was determined to make sure he got the best care I could afford. When we went shopping, I would put him in the cart and he would kneel and face forward. He would say, "Take me fast, Dad." And of course, I would. I'd run up and down the aisles, whipping him around while he giggled. Then I'd slow down to a crawl when there were other shoppers around so no one was the wiser. It was our little secret. We would go to the Fresno Fair and also the amusement park that had carnival rides and a zoo. I would take all of the boys and we would have a blast. It was so much fun.

However, things at home had begun to turn sour. After a while, Lisa and I started fighting. Nothing big at first, but things got pretty heated up after a couple years. Then it became a regular occurrence, fighting about anything or nothing. It seemed like we just wanted to fight so we could make up later. The physical part was excellent for both of us, it always was, but we were fighting practically on a daily basis. One night, she had been drinking and wanted to go to bed and make love. I just didn't want to take a part in that cycle anymore. I was tired of the needless fighting just to make up. It was draining, and I didn't think that was a good example for the boys. After a good half hour of taunting from her, I had enough bullshit and I grabbed my tea glass and threw it. It shattered, and a piece of glass hit her in the leg, carving out a big U-shaped cut in her thigh. She ran into the bedroom and grabbed a sheet to apply pressure to her wound. The sheet was quickly soaked in blood now. I knelt at the bed and said, "I'm calling 911 for an ambulance. Can you just tell them you fell on the glass?"

She said, "You son of a bitch, just make the call." I knew I was a goner then. When the cops got there, they had a conversation with the paramedics on the scene. Then they took us to separate rooms and asked us questions about what had happened. I told them she fell on the broken glass and she told them that I had thrown it at her. I went to jail and that was the beginning of the end for our marriage. She received seventy-five internal and seventy-five external stitches. In retrospect, it was a pretty serious wound.

When I was being processed for jail, the officer asked me if I had ever been an informant. They asked that so they didn't put squealers in the population where they could get hurt by the guys they had snitched on. I said no, but I had worked as a process server for the Fresno County District Attorney's office and there was a good chance I had served papers to a few of the current inmates. That being said, they assigned me to a separate cell. I found out that when an inmate is dressed in orange and has his own cell it meant one of two things. It meant either you were a snitch or a badass. My charges were "assault with a deadly weapon" and "intent to cause bodily harm." For self-preservation, I told everyone I was a badass, but just to be safe, I still gave my bun or single slice of bread to the biggest guy in the joint for protection.

When they asked me why I had my own cell, I played innocent and I said I wasn't sure. Then they asked me what I was charged with and I told them. That seemed to explain it away. I was safe until we got to the arraignment. A bunch of inmates were there, and everyone's charges were read aloud in the courtroom. When the judge got to me, he said, "You caused your wife to receive 150 stiches with a glass . . ." I could hear the other inmates whispering among themselves. I knew I was in trouble. Wife beaters and child molesters were dead meat in the jailhouse. I didn't consider myself a wife beater, but it sure sounded that way on the outside. My bail was set at $10,000 and I thought they must really think they've got something here. Fortunately, Lisa called a bail bondsman and I was out the next day. After that, every time she handed me a glass she would pull it back and say, "You're not going to throw this at me, are you?" She had a sense of humor, but I wanted her to just stop talking about it.

As part of my sentence, I attended anger-management classes and then got a job in Fresno delivering milk. I came home from work one day to find Lisa burning my little notebooks and papers. "What's her name, you son of a bitch?" she screamed as she started throwing cans of pork and beans at me along with everything else that she could grab from the pantry. I dialed 911 and told them my wife was throwing beans at me. The operator chuckled. "Did I hear you correctly, sir? Your wife is throwing beans at you, so you called 911 to report it?"

Yeah, it sounded kind of silly, but it was violence, and after taking those classes, I was trying to avoid any kind of confrontation. "Yes, she's throwing cans of beans and everything else," I said. "Fruits, vegetables, yams, all kinds of things. Listen." I held the phone out and Lisa was cursing up a storm.

"Take that, you son of a bitch!"

"You hear that, ma'am? She's gone crazy. I just got off probation and I can't afford to get in trouble." The cops showed up and asked her if she would just calm down and that we could sleep in separate rooms. I told them I didn't have anywhere else to go and she was the one who had family in the area. They asked her once again if she was going to just let me go to sleep.

"He can sleep, alright," she said, "and if I had a gun, I'd shoot the son of a bitch. That way he can sleep the rest of his life!" They took her to jail and I didn't bail her out until a week later. She ended up losing her job and she went into a rehab center for alcohol addiction.

After both of us had gone to jail because of those epic fights we would have, we realized that we weren't good for each other anymore. Neither of us wanted to go back to jail, and if things continued the way they had been, one of us would end up locked up or dead. It was just best if we went our separate ways. When I broke the sad news to Rob, he cried out, "No, no!" and ran into his room and crawled under the bed. He grabbed the bed legs and wouldn't allow me to pull him out. Lisa and I got down on the floor and we both talked to him until we convinced him to come out from under the bed. He said, "I don't want to get a divorce." Lisa assured him he could come and visit every day if he wanted.

Rob just wanted the family to stay together. He couldn't understand why he was losing his two brothers, the boys he had grown up with. By this time, he was eight years old. He had already lost his real mother and now it was happening again and this time he wasn't only losing "Mama Lisa," but also his best friends. He was devastated, as we all were. I felt bad that I hadn't been able to keep all of us together. He was at a very impressionable age. I just decided that I would try to do everything I could to minimize things.

That was easier said than done because after mom moved out, it was just Rob and me alone again. I had to rely on the kindness of our neighbors to help with babysitting. I left for work at 5:30 in the morning so I could arrive for my shift at 7:00. That meant I had to get Rob up at 5:00 a.m. and get him ready for the day. Then he would sit on the couch and watch cartoons, and when it got light outside, he would walk himself about a mile to the bus stop. The only problem was that he couldn't tell time and he would just leave when he thought it was light enough. Once, I got in trouble for leaving him home alone because he showed up at the bus stop at 6:00 a.m. It was a real struggle, but we made it work. Rob never understood why Lisa and I had divorced and it wasn't something I wanted to talk about. She ended up having an affair with a forest ranger in Yosemite National Park. I couldn't forgive her for being unfaithful to me, and I didn't want Rob to hear all of the messy details.

I could tell that the divorce was hitting Rob really hard. He was depressed in school and started getting in trouble with other students. I came home one day from work and he had broken about one hundred pieces of Spanish tile that I had bought for the kitchen remodeling. I yelled at him and the next day he broke another hundred. I realized that he was lashing out and trying to channel his frustrations, and I wasn't sure what I should do. I made him use his red wagon to move all the broken pieces over to a spot behind the garage, and oddly enough he seemed to enjoy that. I was outside working at the same time and it was sort of an odd bonding moment for us.

Money was tight, and I wasn't sure how I was going to keep the house that we had moved into when there had been five of us. As a solution, I rented out the three bedrooms to local kids in their early twenties. Their portion of the rent helped to make ends meet, which meant that we didn't have to move. To make that work, Rob and I had to sleep on makeshift beds in the dining room. It was not an ideal situation, but work was slow, and I didn't have many options.

Regardless of our home situation, I was dedicated to getting Rob active and involved in as many activities as possible. We did Tiger Scouts, Cub Scouts, Little League baseball, anything he had an interest in. It was my way to keep him busy and to have things that we could do together. I loved attending the meetings and games, being involved in his life. As he got a little older, he entered those difficult years and became a little cocky toward me. I think it was his way of dealing with the changes we had gone through. He probably resented me somewhat for the divorce, but I did what had to be done. When I'd hear him crying at night, I'd try to talk to him, but he would turn his head away from me so that I couldn't see his tears. I understood how he felt and maybe I was selfish for not sticking it out and trying to make the marriage work. It just felt like those violent episodes would continue and that wouldn't be good for anyone. As we slept in the dining room, it reminded me of my dad sleeping in the basement to appear as a regular family, when on the inside we were all messed up. I thought Rob would adjust to the change and from experience I knew it was better than trying to pretend we were a happy family, but it was still difficult.

In May 1999, my mom called and told me that my dad had cancer and the doctor hadn't given him long to live. I realized that I needed to be with my father. I tried to give the house to Lisa, but she said that she couldn't afford the mortgage and taxes. The place was homesteaded so they couldn't foreclose on it for being delinquent on taxes. I worked out a deal where I sold the house to a couple, they made payments to me, and I paid the mortgage company. My mom flew out to California once again and drove my pickup truck back to New York pulling a U-Haul trailer. She also took Rob with her so that she could get him situated and enrolled in school by September. I had so much stuff in that U-Haul and in the bed of the pickup that the headlights pointed up to the sky. I told Mom she couldn't drive at night or in heavy rain because the load wasn't balanced and things could be tricky.

I had to finish up with work and then I flew to New York. As soon as I arrived, I went to my dad's place in Owego and sat with him. He didn't look good at all. He had lost so much weight. When I first saw him, he said, "Kraig, I'm all fucked up. Got a bunch of cancer in me that just won't go away. Thanks for coming. Your mother fixed your old bed up and cleaned your closet out for your clothes."

I was glad to be there for him and neither of us talked much about the past. We were all in the house together and Rob loved being around his grandparents. Mom had enrolled him in Seneca Falls Elementary School, which was near her house. There was a bus stop practically at her front door and that made it very convenient for Rob. I wanted him to go to school near my dad's place, but she didn't think he should be around his sick grandfather all the time. I argued that Dad was still coherent and having his grandson helping him would be a good thing, but I didn't fight it too much. She had done a lot to help us get there and I appreciated the stability she was giving Rob. My dad died October 16, 1999. I had only been able to spend a couple of months with him, but I was glad I had come home.

The next year, I moved Rob to Owego and into a new school. By this time, he was eleven years old and playing pee wee football. He was a defensive end and an offensive guard. Rob was a fantastic player and he knew how to hit hard. Just as I had done with his other activities, I loved going to the games and watching him play. It was such a joy to see my kid chase a runner down and drive him to the ground. Then things started to fall apart again.

Rob and I went on hikes and I took him to all the places in the woods where I had built forts as a kid. I showed him the swimming holes in the creek and all of the secret places I loved as a little boy. As time went on, I discovered that he had been cutting himself. When they discovered that at school, they called an ambulance to take him to the hospital. That was not very common back then, or if it was, it wasn't talked about. I wasn't sure how to deal with it. The doctors weren't much help, but they did think he was acting out because of trouble at home.

I had started seeing an old flame of mine from back in the day. She told me she was getting a divorce, and once we began dating, that's when I discovered the angry slashes on Rob's arms. One time he cut himself so bad that the hospital sent him to psychiatric care. They gave him Thorazine to calm him down. When I went to visit him, he was like a zombie. I knew that wasn't the right place for him so I filled out the papers to get him moved. We had to wait for an open bed in the Elmira Psychiatric Center. I liked that they didn't use heavy drugs as treatment and it seemed like a nice place.

While he was there, Rob took a screw out of a chair in his room and scratched the words "die bitch" on the ceiling. Then he told the nurse to look up when she came to check on him. I took my mom, my girlfriend, and her two daughters to visit him after I got a call from the doctor. There was concern when they found a poem that Rob had written. "I dream of the day when I dance in my father's blood as it rolls down the sidewalk." They told me that before Rob could be released, I would have to get rid of all my guns and other weapons in my house. I had a collection of valuable rifles that had been passed down from my dad. There were over eighteen in total. They meant a lot to me, but naturally my son meant much more so I sold every single one of them.

When Rob was finally able to come home, he was now in his early teens and I knew that this could be a tough time for any kid. I was glad that he played football at school, but he was caught smoking and got kicked off the team. By the time he was fourteen, I was working my own construction business and taking him along to keep him occupied. One time he and I were checking on my concrete crew. I pulled into the job site at a nearby farm and asked him if he wanted to stay in the truck or come with me. I noticed he had tattooed himself with a blue ink pen. It was pretty deep, but I thought he could just wet it and get it off. I told him to have that shit off his hand by the time I got back from checking on the crew or he was going back to Elmira.

When I returned, the pickup truck was gone. I asked the farmhand where my truck was, and he said my kid had driven off with it. I called the cops to help find him and started driving through the backroads where I often gave him driving lessons. The next day, I checked my credit card statement and found a charge for a bag of peanuts at a service station on the Ohio Turnpike. I called around to places in Ohio and then Indiana. I was patched through to the tollbooth where he had been seen.

Apparently, Rob had spent the money I had in my wallet on gas because he first went to the Canadian border. He didn't have ID to go through customs so he headed down 90 and into Ohio. The tollbooth lady said when he didn't have money for the toll, he showed her a driver's license. She took the information down and said, "Have a nice day, Mr. Moss." I told her that was my son and he was fourteen. She said, "He looks old for his age, I guess."

My next call was to the Indiana Highway Patrol. I told them what had happened, and it looked like Rob was headed their way. An Indiana Highway Patrol car pulled up by my truck parked in a service plaza on the turnpike. Rob was inside buying a sandwich, and when he came out to the truck, the trooper said Rob looked at them and sighed. He was wearing his ball cap at a slight angle and talking like a thug. He knew I hated that. The officer said, "What's going on, Rob?"

"Nothing much, just getting a sandwich."

The cop told me he said, "Well, a lot of people are worried about you."

"I'm okay," Rob replied. "I'm not going back to Elmira if that's what you're thinking."

The officer didn't know what he was referring to, but he did know he had found the runaway boy and the truck. They contacted me and agreed to leave the truck at the service plaza. They took Rob to Angola, Indiana, and set a court date, which was two days out. I took off with my now-wife and her youngest daughter. We first went to the service plaza and got my truck. The truck was not smashed up like I had thought it would be. We got to Angola and paid for a motel room. The court hearing was the next morning at 9:00.

The judge entered the courtroom, and everyone stood up except Rob. There he was, slouched in his chair with his arms folded like some punk. The judge said, "Son, you will stand when I enter the courtroom."

Rob muttered, "I'm not your son," as he stood.

"Be seated, please," said the bailiff.

The judge read off some stuff and ordered a psychiatric evaluation on Rob and we were to return in two weeks. He started talking to the district attorney and I spoke up. "Your honor, may I say something?"

The judge looked at me and asked, "Who might you be?"

I replied, "Your honor, I am Rob's father. I took my last vacation days for this year to be at this hearing. I came here with Rob's stepmom and stepsister. I am prepared to return Rob to New York today. I'm not sure how the laws of Indiana work, but if you make him a ward of the state, I can't do anything about it. But I think it's fair to let you know I have no intention of coming back to this court anytime in the near future. In January, I will get a new set of vacation days and could make some plans to visit at that time. I just want you to know you will be completely responsible for him for the next four to five months."

"I see," said the judge. "Well, I guess we better adjourn for lunch and we will meet back in this courtroom in two hours. Court is adjourned."

In light of the circumstances that the truck was stolen from the state of New York and the minor was not apprehended actually driving the truck, the judge leaned forward and said, "I guess we have a good idea as to how the truck got to the service plaza, but we have no proof now, do we? The State of Indiana will not charge Rob J. Moss and will release the minor to his family who came here from New York. Now Mr. Moss, you be sure to call this court and let me know when you have arrived back home. Is that understood?"

Back in New York, I started having Rob work with me on weekends. He showed interest in learning how to operate the different kinds of equipment I owned—bulldozer, excavator, backhoe, skid steer, whatever it was he was a quick learner and he soon became a big part of the business. We went together on estimates, and by the time he was seventeen, he was capable of setting up concrete forms and getting things ready for a concrete pour. He could run a crew the day of the pour as well. I remember one time I took Rob fishing down to the Susquehanna River that ran through Apalachin and Owego where we lived. I showed Rob how to put a number three hook in the tail of a crayfish. We put the hook in the tail so it could crawl on the floor of the river. The hook under the skin of the tail would release the smell of the crayfish. Then a big ole carp would come by and gobble it up, hook and all.

"We got one, Rob! Reel him in," I would say, then I'd hand him the pole. A river carp with a ten-pound test line using a pond pole is like catching a blue marlin in the ocean. It's a real fight and you have to help it to shore until you get him close. It felt good to have an activity that we shared and enjoyed other than work.

I was not happy when Rob announced that he wanted to quit school and go to California. His mom, who had been absent most of his life, had promised him the world if he came out there. Time and again, she had disappointed him, but he kept giving her another chance with the hopes that things would be different. He soon found out that the grass was not greener, and he returned to New York and finished up at the same high school that I had graduated from in 1977. I was so proud of him. He did this on his own without me bitching at him.

Rob fell back into his work routine with me on the weekends and made good money. He bought a 1987 Monte Carlo SS and after his graduation he worked for me full time and we did everything together. We traveled to auctions and worked on our construction equipment. I remember once I was pulling him with my dump truck. He was steering a bread van that was chained to the truck. As we got going down a hill, I gunned it and caused him to smash into the back of the dump truck. He cussed me out something terrible when we got stopped and then we both just broke out laughing. "You fucker," he said, gasping for air. "That scared the shit out of me, Pop!"

I said, "Ah, it's all good. I'm hungry, let's get something to eat."

"Where we going?" he asked.

"I thought we would go check out that new all-you-can-eat Chinese place that just opened up."

Rob responded with a smile, "All you can eat Chinese? Sweet, let's go."

By now Rob had pretty much lost the tough-guy attitude and I was happy for that. He also was wearing his John Deere hat straight forward and not sideways, which was a sign of maturity in my book. Rob had really grown into a wonderful young man and helped the neighbors all the time. He would go around in the winter and shovel snow, making up to $500 in four hours. If they said they couldn't afford to pay him, he would just smile at them and tell them not to worry about it. As a father, I was proud of him and happy to see that he had matured and grown out of that difficult adolescent phase. I just wanted to have a good, strong relationship with him and help him become a good man. It seemed like he was finally on the right path.

One day we were working on a job site when the phone rang. It was Rob's mom. "What's up?" I asked. I didn't need for her to stir anything up.

"Just let me talk to my son, please."

After the call, Rob sat down and started to cry. I asked him what was wrong, and he pushed me away and turned his head. He then looked up at me and cried, "Derrick is dead. My brother Derrick is dead." Apparently, he had died the night before when a car he was driving slammed sideways into a palm tree in Pasadena. Derrick was the only one killed, but there were three others in the car who were seriously injured. Rob had talked to him and Jack on a regular basis and they really got along well. I made arrangements for Rob to fly to California and attend his brother's funeral, not realizing how much it would affect him.

I had gotten a divorce the year Rob graduated from high school. Of course, Jo-an came to the graduation ceremony, but it just wasn't the same. Rob had a few girlfriends along the way, but all of his relationships seemed to end up in a dramatic scene with yelling and doors slamming. Once I was talking about the things my wives had done and Rob piped up and said, "Oh, it's always someone else's fault isn't it, Pop? Did you ever think just maybe it could be you and your yelling bullshit, huh? Did you ever think just maybe after three wives that it might be you, oh great one?"

I guess I deserved that, but I just wasn't ready for it. I had done the best I could, but it just never seemed to be enough. No matter how many good times we had and memories we shared, the bad times always seemed to outweigh everything else. He held on to things and couldn't let go. I understood that life was tough, and I hadn't made all the right decisions, but who does? We all do the best that we can. That's what I was trying to teach him. We make mistakes, we screw up, but then we keep on going and hopefully do better next time.

Any time he would lash out like that, it never dawned on me that he could be under some kind of influence. Now it makes sense because they would seemingly come from out of nowhere. It was odd that he would bring negative things up even when we were having a good time. It was almost like he wanted to sabotage things because that felt normal. When we got into those fights, my mind would immediately go back to the fun times we had. We would even make mundane chores like shopping an adventure. After we'd get paid, we would get seven shopping carts and fill them with whatever food we wanted. We would just go crazy, no questions asked. We would fish from the banks of the local rivers, take our boat out on Cayuga Lake to go water skiing, and take camping trips out west to Yosemite or Bass Lake in California. We went to several different amusement parks like Magic Mountain, Disneyworld, and Disneyland.

I often think back on the past and I recognize now that the time I spent with Rob was good enough to satisfy me, but maybe it wasn't good enough for him. He needed me all the time and I wished I had been able to stay married. I can't understand why I did so much to disrupt our family life. I started out with good intentions and then messed it up somehow.

Maybe my dad was right. Maybe I could fuck up a free lunch.

8

AT BLINDING SPEED

By the fall of 2016, the presidential campaign was in full swing. It was a matchup between Donald Trump and Hillary Clinton. I had been campaigning for Trump for so long that it just seemed like a foregone conclusion. He would be the president. There was never a question in my mind nor the minds of folks at those rallies. Everyone saw the grassroots effort, the true passion that these hard-working regular folks felt for Trump. Obviously, they would influence their friends and it would continue to spread. We were all ready for some kind of change and this man seemed to represent that.

We all knew that he was rich and powerful, something we would never experience, but as we watched him fumble and stumble through the political process, we could see ourselves in him. He was direct, crass, imperfect, and human. He wasn't a typical polished politician saying the right things at the right time. Hell, he often said things that we didn't like or agree with, but no one ever agrees with a candidate 100 percent. That's just not practical.

On the other hand, there was Hillary Clinton and on the campaign trail I was often asked by supporters and the news media why I didn't support her given she most likely would have adopted a healthcare bill that could have provided coverage and services for all Americans including those affected by addiction. I would tell them that it was plain and simple. I just didn't like her and still don't. That meant I didn't believe her and I couldn't stand to hear her squawking, irritable voice. I realized maybe that was superficial, but I had to go with my gut. My instincts were telling me that she would not represent me and my community.

I do think that news outlets and social media probably had a lot to do with my opinion. The Whitewater scandal and the stock futures investment episodes gave me a sour taste about her. All the controversy surrounding Vince Foster and his suicide really made me cringe. I felt like I couldn't believe a word she said and the whole Benghazi fiasco is what put me over the edge. It was possibly the one comment from Hillary about her negligence or disregard to internal requests for added security in Benghazi, specifically for the people who lost their lives, when she said, "What difference does it make." To me she was making light of the investigation. No apology, no remorse, and no admission of knowledge of any written warnings about the situation, yet to me it was proven there were indeed multiple requests for added security.

The list of lies and activities from this corrupt, seasoned politician seemed to walk a fine line just this side of legal, and that never sat right with me. Hillary Clinton to me represented the stereotypical political figure. Her denial of sending classified emails and playing dumb, as I saw it, just made me sick. On one hand, she claimed to be this bright promising attorney who was tuned into the needs of the American people, and on the other, she portrayed herself as an innocent victim who just couldn't understand the problems of regular people. After all, "Others have used their phones and insecure sites to receive and send classified material," she said.

I suppose part of my distrust for Hillary stems from her husband's testimony under oath that he "did not engage in sexual activity with that woman." However, very little weight goes into my opinion of her from this and other lies the former president told. The name Clinton certainly was amplified in my head due to those testimonies and others related to her husband's time in office. The constant investigations and seemingly corrupt happenings around her on a regular basis throughout her political career led me to believe, even though much is speculation or hasn't been proven, that I had to put myself in the category of "never Hillary." It may be unfair, but people such as Hillary Clinton, career politicians who now and again turn their heads on ethical decision-making to benefit their own personal gain, are the exact reason I had never voted before the 2016 election.

They are all crooks. I was one of the many who was affected by Donald Trump's admission that he was not a politician. Trump had, in my opinion, proven he was not of the same mold as every other politician who was capable of looking you in the eye and telling you what you wanted to hear to get your vote. Trump's raw, unrehearsed, and unscripted style of delivery was the very ingredient that myself and millions of Americans became addicted to. We found it refreshing.

Having such a stark difference in candidates, to many Americans it was an obvious choice. We were ready for someone who wasn't overly rehearsed and practiced and perfect. What we saw in our candidate was someone who could screw up and keep on going. He was like us and that motivated many people who had never even voted before to register and support him as our president.

During my trip across the United States for the primary race, I heard all of the poll results by the media and I never trusted them. I mean, I guess if you get the right people participating you can get any result you want, but like I said, there were many of us who had never even voted before so I'm sure that we were not counted and that was a real mistake. I told everyone when Trump was in Indiana and the polls had Cruz ahead by 12 percent not to believe the numbers posted by the media. I wrote on my Facebook page and told all my Trump friends, and all those anti-Trump friends as well, not to believe the numbers touted by the media. Everywhere I went, there were Trump signs galore. About seven out of every ten people I met on the road were voting for Trump. There was no question that these people were not being counted. Once again, they were overlooked, not by politicians but by pollsters and the media. That was a mistake.

Those ridiculous poll numbers just helped to strengthen Trump's stance that you couldn't trust the media. You couldn't trust the system and the system is rigged. It made everything Trump was saying true and it validated all of his brutal verbal exchanges with members of the media at the rallies. We now had evidence that what the media was saying just wasn't true. We were there on the ground every single day.

I went into a restaurant in Denison, Iowa, and sat at a table in the middle of the place. I would always carry my guitar inside and put three or four Trump CDs on the edge of my table. I would hold one up as if reading the songs and make sure people saw what I had. "Where did you get that?" someone would invariably ask.

"Oh, it's a Trump CD that I made," I'd say nonchalantly. Then the diners would launch into a political discussion about the candidates, always favoring Trump.

"You go ahead and vote for Cruz, but Trump's the man that's going to turn things around in this country."

"Oh yeah, I heard he's going to make America great again. You go ahead and keep believing that, you ole fart!"

By that time, it was clear who the Trump supporters were. I would go back to my truck and grab more CDs because I was selling them right and left after that. It was encounters like those that let me know Trump was more popular than the media wanted us to think. That was Iowa and he wasn't doing very well there in real time, but he held his own.

I could take an informal poll by driving around and seeing the political signs. I would see the professionally made, oversized "Trump for President" signs in front of businesses and smaller ones stabbed into the grassy yards of every neighborhood. There were even homemade Trump signs in city squares and on the corners of country roads. Donald J. Trump had made his mark in America and no matter how hard the media tried to twist things, he was doing very well.

I returned home from the Manchester rally and voted on November 8. I watched the news try to convince us that Trump was going to fail, and Hillary R. Clinton would be the next president of the United States. I laughed. I had people on Facebook ask me if I was sure about what I'd seen on my journey across the United States and I assured them. "You better believe it!" I posted. I was on the ground talking to everyday Americans in cities all across the country and I heard the emotional cries of help from all of them. It was undeniable.

He's not a politician, they would say, *and it's about time someone got in Washington and cleaned house.* "Drain the swamp," as Trump said. I heard, saw, and felt the emotions of the American people and it wasn't in support of Hillary. I mean, it wasn't even close. There were never any proud Clinton supporters where I went. Now, I didn't go to downtown Chicago, for instance, but I was in every small county from New York to California and what I saw was a movement for a change and that change was Donald J. Trump. No question.

On the night of the election, I went to bed around 8:30 and when I awoke it was no surprise to me that Donald J. Trump was elected president of the United States. My phone rang off the wall with requests for interviews from every newspaper and foreign media outlets. Everyone I had met on the road or who had read one of the articles about me wanted my opinion. They wanted to know how I had been so confident about a Trump presidency. They also wanted to understand how the polls had been so wrong. They wanted answers about this whole group of people they didn't understand.

Mr. Trump had worked hard for this position and it seemed the more people tried to smear his name, the more popular he became. Once I asked an older lady, probably in her late seventies, what she thought of the latest Trump controversy. She replied, "Oh, what's he said now that's got everyone buzzing? Who cares what he said? I like him and I'm going to vote for him. We need a change in Washington. They have robbed us for the last time. Trump's going to drain the swamp!"

This was the sentiment across the country. No one cared what he had said and when the media tried to make a big deal out of something. It just helped prove Trump's accusations that they were out to get him with their fake news.

9

INTO THE NIGHT

Back in 2003, I pulled my big rig to the side of the road at the Delaware Water Gap because I suddenly felt sick. I climbed out of the cab and made my way to the side of the road. I clutched the grass feeling like I was being pulled away from the earth. I threw up, coughing and spitting like crazy. I was dizzy and feeling like I just wanted to stay on the side of the road. I sat there for an hour or so, then climbed into the cab and made my way to the terminal. Two months went by before I found out through my stepdaughter that Rob had put rat poison in my coffee in an attempt to kill me. He apparently was upset that I kept him from going to a school dance because he had forty-five missing assignments from school.

Ten years later, Rob and I had tons of business and we were doing things together outside of the workplace. How things had changed. By that time, Rob and I were getting along great. We would often go into reminiscing about living in California and when we first moved back to the East Coast. We laughed about me giving Rob a ride on my four-wheeler in the snow and the neighbor was outside trying to stop us by waving us down. It seemed we were riding on his property a little and his wife was in the doorway holding the phone in the air to let us know she was calling the police. "That man wants us to stop, Dad," twelve-year-old Rob said.

"Just hold on and don't look at him. Pretend he is not there," I instructed as my son laughed at our antics. We had so many good times and often talked

137

about them. In July 2013, I had gone to bed early. We had to work the next morning and I was concerned that Rob hadn't made it home yet. He had started going to downtown Owego and hanging out with a much darker type crowd. I mean, they were just strange. That's the best way I can describe them as they wore oversized hats like some kind of Mad Hatter gang. One kid would wear a Patriots hat like from the 1700s. Many wore hoodies and that was often Rob's outfit of choice.

That's the night that I woke from a deep sleep to a loud screeching noise and banging. I got up to look out the window. Just as I reached the front door, it opened and there was Rob standing in the doorway with blood covering his face and soaking into his sweatshirt. "Holy shit, Rob, what the hell happened?" I asked as I grabbed him by his shoulder and pulled him into the house and closed the door. "What the hell happened?" I asked while I led him up the stairs to the hall that went into the bathroom.

He said, "I got into a wreck coming into Owego. I got a flat tire and spun out of control."

I noticed his words were slurred and I asked, "How much have you had to drink?"

"No, I haven't been drinking," he replied.

"Come on, Rob, you smashed your car and can't talk without slurring your words," I called out while inspecting his head and wiping the blood from the three-inch long, half-inch deep cut on his head.

"Swear to God, Pop, I wasn't drinking."

"Okay, well hold this towel right here on your head. I'll be right back."

"What are you going to do?" he asked.

"I'm going to get your car out back and cover it up. If the cops see it, they will know it was you. Was there anybody else involved?"

"No."

"Was there anyone with you?"

"No, Pop. Just me."

I went outside and walked around the car really quick. The rear bumper was missing and the entire driver's side was smashed in. I couldn't understand how the door still functioned. The right front was smashed in, but it looked like the radiator was still intact. I drove the car around the back of my house. The right rear tire was flat, but it was drivable. Wow, I couldn't believe he made it through downtown Owego without being pulled over. The license plate was mounted on the trunk lid so they couldn't trace the wreck to him. I covered the car with a blue tarp. My one neighbor was on vacation and the other had turned on their back-porch light due to the commotion, but no one had come outside. I slipped into the house through the side door that led into the garage. In the downstairs area, up the two flights of stairs, I went to the bathroom where Rob was calmly sitting down and holding the towel to his head.

"What am I going to do?" he asked.

"I don't know. We are going to look at this cut first," I said.

"My car is ruined," he moaned, and he started crying. "I'm sorry, Pop. I messed up big time. I love you, Pop. You always help me, and I always fuck up somehow."

I said, "You just be still and let me look at this cut." I pulled his hair left and right to expose the deep cut. "This thing needs stitches for sure," I said while I sat on the edge of the bathtub. Rob was sitting on the toilet seat with the seat down. He was sobbing, and I lifted his chin up with my hand, looked him in the eye, and said, "You don't worry about that car, you hear? You can buy another one. The question is, what do you want to do? If you go to the hospital, they are going to ask questions and the news of the wreck with auto parts all over the road is likely to make the scanners. You got two choices. You can either go to the hospital and take your chances they don't figure out it was you that hit the bridge in Owego and left the scene or I can doctor this thing up myself. It's not life threatening and I'm pretty sure I can mend you up good enough to heal on its own."

"Go ahead and fix it for me, Pop," he said as he continued to cry. I opened up the medicine cabinet and pulled out the half-used tube of triple antibiotic. I had already used the first half of it on my cat Digger when he tangled with a possum and lost. I was going to cut some of Rob's hair back but was afraid of getting dirt in the wound. I squeezed a bunch of the gel directly into the cut. Then I put the rest over the top and in his hair around the cut. Slowly, I twisted the hair from one side of the cut to the hair on the other side of the cut. His hair was only a few inches long, but it twisted together nicely. I finished pulling the cut closed. I told him to sleep on the opposite side and we would keep an eye on it to make sure it didn't become infected. In less than a week, the wound began to scab over and I was glad to see no signs of infection.

It had rained on and off after the accident, so by the time the scabbing started, we were ready to go back to work. Rob talked to his friends and told them of his wreck. They already knew about it because somebody Rob knew saw the cops in the road picking up pieces of his car and putting them in a Village of Owego maintenance truck.

We continued to work together, but that night stuck in my head. Rob had been crying, but now I wasn't so sure it had been because he was distraught about crashing his car. Something just didn't add up. However, he stuck to his commitment and continued to make payments to the neighbor who sold him the car. That was one of his qualities that I was proud of; he would always follow through on a promise. He knew he owed money to our neighbor Ed who had sold him the car on a handshake. Ed even went ahead and signed over the title to Rob while he continued making monthly payments. Rob managed to honor his debt even though the car was totaled, and he only had liability insurance. There was no way to salvage it, but he had to pay that one off before he could even think about a replacement.

When I think back to that accident, I remember that Rob kept telling me he was sorry. I consoled him, but I just couldn't figure out exactly what he was sorry about. Now, after taking in everything, I began to wonder if he was sorry for getting hooked on heroin. This was something we talked about all the time as he was growing up. I knew he drank and smoked pot, but hell I did that stuff too when I was his age and managed to stay out of trouble. Now that I know Rob was into heroin, maybe he was crying out an apology for messing up as he said that night. He wasn't upset about the car at all. He was apologizing for getting into heroin when he promised me he would never do that stuff.

It makes sense because I'm sure he was telling the truth then about not drinking. What I came to realize later is that he must have been high on heroin at that point. Based on his mannerisms and his slurring, something was affecting him. I hadn't smelled any alcohol, but back then I didn't even think about other drugs. It just didn't cross my mind that he could have been strung out because I had no idea that he was using. I was clueless. Thinking back, I just wish I could have picked up on some sign or clue. Maybe he was trying to tell me, hoping I would figure it out and confront him. We usually had such an open relationship that we talked about everything. If he was dealing with addiction, I just wished he could have confided in me and asked for help. Then we might have had a fighting chance. We might have avoided the inevitable.

Rob brought his girlfriend over to the house once in a while and I often wonder if I did the right thing letting her stay in his room. I knew what they were doing. I had grown strong with the Lord by that time and I just let it go. I found out later that summer she was a heroin addict. Rob found needles in her purse and threw her and her belongings out in the street, telling her to get out and never come back. When I found out why he kicked her out of the house, I was so proud of him and never ever suspected he was using heroin as well. Two days went by, and that's when he confided in me that he had smoked heroin before, but did not like it. I should have taken action at that point. I should have been more vigilant, but somehow, I turned my head and said to myself, *it's going to be okay. If Rob says he's not hooked then I believe him.*

Things seemed to level out and our regular lives resumed until news came through one of his friends that a guy we knew had killed himself with a 38-caliber handgun. He had been using heroin and just broken up with his girlfriend. He was depressed and apparently felt there was no other answer. I went to the funeral with Rob because he had been one of the guys Rob would bring over to help with a concrete pour or other odd jobs. The guy was going to college and worked with us now and again when he was home from school on break.

Two weeks after that, another of Rob's friends was found hanging by a rope in her bedroom. She and Rob had even dated casually, but it never turned into anything serious. It came to light that she had also experimented with heroin, Rob told me, "but she wasn't an addict." I didn't say anything, but once you dabble with that stuff, you're basically an addict. It's not debatable. Then I was stunned when yet another one of Rob's friends died from a heroin overdose. His parents owned the funeral home that took care of the services for my mom and dad. Over the next few months, we heard about a couple of other incidents regarding drugs.

I was witness to my community becoming engulfed in drugs and addiction. It happened so gradually at first that it just seemed like random events, but it was a snowball effect. More and more stories came out about local people, usually young folks, who had become addicted to heroin and then overdosed or killed themselves in another way to escape the addiction. I think the community was in shock. We certainly were not equipped to handle these tragedies emotionally or from a preventative standpoint. It was new to us and we didn't have the tools to fight this invisible war. Our children and our friends' children were being taken from us at an increasingly rapid pace and we could only stand by, helpless and confused.

Last year when Trump basically said *believe me because I'm going to fix the problems that are important to you,* I should have realized that something wasn't right. There was no way he could do all of the things he had promised. It's strange to think that the reason I followed Trump around was because I thought he could help with the drug problem that had taken my son away. And in doing so, I ended up trusting Trump and his promises just as I had trusted my son when he told me he was clean. In both cases, I should have pushed back, asked more questions, and worked harder to get to the truth. It's important to show trust, but that wasn't enough in either instance. There was too much at stake with Rob and Trump. My blind trust just gave them both the freedom to do what they wanted to do. For Rob, it ended with him taking his own life. With Trump, it led to a world of chaos and broken promises.

I talked to Rob about all of the people dying around him and he just passed it off. He was mostly upset about his ex-girlfriend hanging herself. I know she wanted to get back with Rob at one time, but he had found the redhead by then and moved on with his life. All these people dying around Rob couldn't be healthy. His main friends had become a group that hung around in the local town. He didn't hang around any of his old teammates from football or baseball. I felt like this new crowd was bad news and they weren't just twenty-year-olds, but some older folks too. The drug really doesn't discriminate when it comes to age or income.

Rob and I were getting ready for a concrete pour one day when he got a call from a friend of his. Rob left the job site about 3:30 p.m. I asked him if everything was okay and he said, yeah, he just needed to do a favor for a friend. I said, "Okay, remember we've got a concrete pour here tomorrow at noon."

"Yeah, I know, don't worry, Pop."

I looked at him and said, "Don't mess me up now, I need you tomorrow." He assured me everything was okay, and he would bring his buddy to help pour the walls.

The favor as it turned out was for Rob to drive two guys to New York City. Of course, I wasn't aware of what the favor was until after it had happened. I found out Rob had driven his friends to the city to visit someone. Now that I knew what everyone had been into, I'm sure it was a drug run. They were supposed to go down and be back for the pour, but I had to cancel the job when they hadn't shown up. Rob didn't answer his phone, so I went in search of him and located him at his pal's trailer. He said he drove his friends to the city to visit someone and they almost got car-jacked. They stopped at a bank in Newburg, New York, on the way back and tried to cash a check that the guy had gotten from his sister. The bank wouldn't cash the check because he didn't have an account there, but apparently the teller felt sorry for them and lent them $20 of her own money for gas so they could get home. I was so mad. I lost it.

"You promised me, you son of a bitch! What the hell were you thinking?" I screamed at the top of my lungs. I was pissed.

He never raised a voice and said in a relaxed, mellow voice, "Calm down, Pop. We'll pour your precious concrete tomorrow."

That made me even madder because it seemed like he was minimizing his responsibility. I took my work and my commitments seriously and I had taught him to do the same thing, so I didn't like that he was so cavalier about it. I had calmed down by the next day when they showed up and we poured the walls for our customers. I took them out for dinner and paid the part-timers in cash for their work.

It was December 2013 when Rob and I were working on that huge foundation job. We were replacing all four walls of the old farmhouse. It was very dangerous work as we had to excavate under a portion of the home that never had a basement in it. Rob would bring his friends to work now and again, including the one he had driven to NYC, the same one who it turned out was a contributing factor in Rob's death. All of my workers would benefit whenever the draws came through and we got paid. I noticed Rob was always broke these days. He used to save his money and now he kept lending any extra funds he had to his friends. Most of his new friends didn't seem to have a job and would work only when Rob asked them to help on a concrete pour. This was mostly because I paid them cash for the day and they didn't have to pee in a cup for a hiring process.

CHAPTER 9

I was so proud on Christmas Eve when Rob and I worked on the job way into the dark. We quit about 9:30, long after the sun had gone down, but I never told him that I was proud of him. I know that was important for him to hear, but I never said it to him. Once when he was five or so, he took a huge poop and left it in the toilet to show me when I got home from work. He grabbed me by my hand and pulled me into the bathroom, pointing at his accomplishment and saying, "You proud of me, Dad?"

As hard as Rob worked that holiday, I feel so bad that we didn't even have a Christmas tree at home; both of us were just trying to patiently wait for the next check to come in. We were supposed to get twenty inches of snow starting Christmas morning. We worked fast to cover up the drain pipe and septic lines. We back-filled along the newly poured concrete walls and got everything ready for the impending snowfall. I was so proud of my son. He worked by my side and never complained one bit. We received our next draw and Rob got $3,000 for his efforts. I asked him if he wanted me to hold on to some of his money for him and he told me, "No, that's okay, Pop, I'm good." His friend got $2,000 and they both were very happy and ran off to celebrate.

Rob's buddy was an excellent worker and would work late hours with Rob and me if we asked him to in order to prepare for an early morning concrete pour. I found out that Rob had gotten his lethal dose of fentanyl-laced heroin from a local dealer and his buddy was the one who had picked it up for him. The night before Rob died, he had been at his friend's rundown trailer on the edge of town. It was one of those 1950s-looking tin cans that smelled of mold and trouble. His friend had injected Rob with a shot of heroin the night of January 5, 2016. I found out later that Rob had overdosed at the trailer, but he and another friend were able to pound his chest and bring him back somehow. Rob came home late and went straight to bed. The next morning, I spoke to Rob for the last time as I headed out the door for work at my new job at the gas company. It was January 6, 2014. Rob's friend had explained to Rob that the reason he was sick was because he needed more heroin, but the truth came out later that Rob's body was breaking down and he needed medical treatment, not more heroin. Oddly enough, that friend and his girlfriend have a child that was addicted to heroin and they named him Rob.

I talked to Rob about his choice of new friends all the time, but I couldn't get anywhere with him. Maybe I didn't try hard enough. He would remind me how I taught him not to judge people by their skin color, religion, or possessions. He reminded me of this and I said, "I know, but these people you're hanging around with are just bad news." What was I to do? I needed him to work with me because he knew everything and could run the jobs himself. I was concerned about his activities, but he was an adult and he kept assuring me that everything was okay.

I should have known and recognized there was a problem, but when Rob worked, he was spot-on and reliable. I put all of the blame on his friends. They were the problem, and they were the reason for him messing up. I never even considered that my son could be contributing to his own tragic end. It was a difficult position to be in. I tried to respect my son and show him that I trusted him, but I also wanted to be his father, to shake him and say, "You have to listen to me and do what I tell you to do."

Not taking more action will always play on my mind. While I'm driving on those long, lonely open roads, I often think back to all of the times when I could have put my foot down and enforced my house rules. I should have worried less about how he would react and more about how he might not be around if I didn't do something drastic. I'm not sure it would have made any difference. In fact, I'm pretty sure that it wouldn't have, but at least I would have tried.

Now all I'm left with are the memories of what a good boy he was and how proud I was of him. I'm left with thoughts of whether or not I was right for taking him away from his mom. I will always wonder if I hadn't divorced my wives, maybe things might have been different. Now that I think of the Indiana deal and the stealing of my truck, that moment in court that I basically told the judge I was going to leave my child to the courts and not come back for a long time if they were to keep him. I wonder if that played on Rob's mind. It all doesn't really matter now I suppose. He's dead, but I'm the one living in hell each and every day.

10

LET'S MAKE AMERICA
GREAT AGAIN

Election day came and went. Just as I had told all the people I had been talking to, Donald J. Trump would be our new president. I had gone to bed early on election night already comforted by the fact that he would win with no problem, even though the media continued to tout Clinton as the early victor. With his presidency on the horizon, I just waited for Trump to come through on his promises.

In January 2017, Trump started out working hard in the White House. He was signing executive orders on the very day of his inauguration. I didn't agree with every issue Trump campaigned on during the election and hadn't changed my mind now. The only difference was that things were happening. He was actually in office and executing his plans just as he had told all of us on the campaign trail. He signed the order that was referred to as "a ban on Muslims" right off. He listed seven countries with terrorist ties or known to have aided terrorists somehow in the past by allowing them to hide in their country, but we all knew what he was doing. The circuit courts figured it out real quick and put a hold on everything. Trump's deportation policy was being enforced as well. It made me cringe every time I saw footage of families being torn apart and children being sent to social services while their mom and dad were deported back to Mexico or whatever country was their origin.

I put on blinders in regard to these happenings and many more because I still believed in the cause. I still held tight to the fact that the man himself had given me his word. Trump had promised to do everything in his power to fight the opioid crisis. He promised me personally at that January 15 rally in Urbandale, Iowa. "In honor of your son, we're going to fight this heroin problem and help these kids get off this terrible drug. Believe me!" I have come to understand now that if a man has to remind you that you can trust him, well that's a red flag and you should probably reconsider.

As for my agenda and the promises, I was waiting for President Trump to come through and I figured it was just a matter of time. I didn't even pay much attention to what he was doing. The news was filled with the 9th Circuit Court having hearings, but that didn't affect or deter me. I was selfish during the campaign and I was selfish after. I have no problem admitting that. My main focus was on one thing—healthcare in this country and the inclusion of provisions to provide services for those addicted to opiates like heroin, OxyContin, and related drugs. I was just waiting and savoring the fact that Donald J. Trump was now the president and I had been around the country promoting him during his campaign. I couldn't imagine how many thousands of people I had spoken to, touting the qualities that Mr. Trump would bring to the Oval Office. I was sure that he was the very best man for the job and I shared that message with many, many people.

After his win, I was contacted by some of my so-called friends telling me, "I hope you're happy now that you helped get this maniac into office," or "You should be ashamed of yourself for supporting this jerk." Whatever it was, I took it lightly as I knew many were bitter and couldn't believe what had happened. This nonpolitician had reached out to the American people and through surveys and polls had found the very issues that we were all passionate about. As it turned out, Trump's team led a brilliant campaign. After they sent out these lengthy surveys, they sent individual promotions including the very issues you were concerned with in the survey. For instance, I was interested in the heroin problem in the survey so any emails I would receive included in detail Trump's promise to fight the heroin problem. If you wanted better healthcare for the veterans, your emails would include detailed information on how he would help the veterans and so on . . . just like that. Trump simply asked people what they wanted most and promised he would do it. Healthcare, heroin crises, veterans' issues, NAFTA, deportation, the wall, protect our country at all cost, get rid of the bad eggs, keep jobs in America, develop urban renewal, create jobs for the jobless, give homes to the homeless, stop senseless spending in Washington, help America before we lend a hand to others, make everyone pay their fair share for protection by the United States, ban Muslims, and so on. Whatever your survey indicated was important to you, he directed promises back to your email on that very subject. And it worked.

That's one of the many ways Trump grabbed so many supporters and votes. He got all those folks in the country outside of the big cities to get up and vote, and they showed up in overwhelming numbers. It's funny how Trump cried during the entire 2016 campaign how the election was rigged and there was so much corruption involved that "the honest man," and I assume he was referring to himself, didn't have a chance. Turns out if it wasn't for the electoral system, he wouldn't have been elected. I guess that's why he's not trying to change that particular process.

After the election, my mantra was "life is good." I boasted to so many how President Trump was going to make a difference in this country. "You just wait and see," I would tell the nonbelievers who were now grumbling about this Russian thing. At first, I was embarrassed when President Trump accused the Obama administration of wiretapping Trump Towers. I said to myself, "not again." We had the birth certificate and other accusations of corruption, and now Trump Towers was bugged. I did hear that they had bugged Paul Manafort's phone lines and that directly was a tie to the Trump campaign, but at this point I'm not sure what to believe.

As far as the Hillary Clinton emails that were exposed prior to the election, if there was no damaging information in those emails, it wouldn't have been a big deal. Turns out the emails showed just how much of a liar Hillary actually was and how she was no different than any other politician by manipulating people with calculated strategy. There has been one thing after another about Hillary and her lies that just soured me. I did like the way Elizabeth Warren fought for a healthcare bill that would help all Americans, but as soon as she hooked up with Hillary Clinton, I had looked the other way and jumped on the Trump Train.

By mid-February 2017, I was working out of Ohio on the gas fields. I was getting ready to go home and put on a small fundraiser for the local nonprofit organization called Trinity CASA. They help heroin addicts get treatment and educate fifth, sixth, and seventh graders on the dangers of using drugs. The concert was called "The Rob Moss Heroin Awareness Tour" and we were scheduled to play March 11, 2017. I was sitting in my hotel room in Newcomerstown, Ohio, when the phone rang. "Is this Kraig Moss?" the voice on the other end asked. I responded yes, and she identified herself as the secretary for Elizabeth Cohen from CNN. She asked me how I felt about President Trump wanting to take $6.5 billion away from existing programs currently in place to treat those addicted to heroin and other opiates. I told her I didn't know that to be true and just because she told me it was true didn't mean that I was going to believe her. We talked a little more and I told her I was going to look into the matter. It seems the content of the new health-care bill had just been released minutes before she called me.

A week had gone by and I received calls from several other news outlets asking me about President Trump's attempt to disrupt opiate treatment programs that the Obama administration had put in place. It wasn't until I received a call back from CNN that I was educated enough on the proposed healthcare bill that I could talk intelligently on the subject. I told the woman at CNN that I had read the inclusions of the proposed bill and frankly I was disgusted as to its content. "This is not at all what President Trump promised me or the American people." That's all the woman needed to hear, and she started asking me about my availability in the near future. I told her I was planning a return to New York to put on a benefit in Rob's name on March 11. We talked about where that would be and how we were going to be able to get together for an on-camera interview. We settled on March 13 as I would need a day to tear down my equipment and assist the people in removing the equipment.

A huge snowstorm arrived on the thirteenth, dropping thirty inches in our area just west of Binghamton, New York, along the Pennsylvania border. I was now being contacted by Elizabeth Cohen herself and she told me her flight into the area had been canceled. They arrived the next day, March 14, and the wind was blowing fiercely. Elizabeth called me and told me they had landed safely, and we would be meeting the next morning at the place where I held the benefit. I told her she was a brave soul to fly in such dangerous conditions. I told her about something we use in the gas fields called "stop work authority" where if any individual sees an unsafe condition they can issue a stop work authority until the dangerous condition is remedied. She laughed and said she didn't think her boss would ever recognize this kind of self-initiated stop work thing, but she might look into it for future use.

CNN came and filmed an interview with me about my travels and asked if I had stopped supporting President Trump. "He lied to me, plain and simple," I responded. "He told me he was going to do everything in his power to make healthcare more affordable, with lower deductibles, lower overall cost, and better coverage. His fight would include the development of more treatment centers and rehabilitation programs for the addicted. The truth of the matter was that he was cutting $300 million from one program and $250 million from another and taking away $6.5 billion from Medicaid, which would basically eliminate the program. One out of every four Americans on Medicaid receives treatment for opiate addiction." We continued with the interview and I just told the truth on how I felt about the lies President Trump made to me and the American people.

Later on, I was a guest on *The Erin Burnett Show*, and made at least seven other appearances on CNN for this show or another. I was contacted one time by Fox News. They wanted me as a guest that afternoon in New York, but I was working so I couldn't make it. I was pretty busy for a while making time for Erica Hill and all the travels for that show. Jake Tapper contacted me and had me on as a guest. That was one of the most emotional interviews I did as I described what kind of person my son Rob was. I broke down during the interview, but they showed it anyway. Jake also got emotional, but he did well to hold back the tears. I was not so successful, I'm afraid.

Then Kate Bolduan called me and I was on her show. I did *New Day with Steve Forrest* and some kind of one-hundred-day report card for President Trump on CNN as well. I was on MSNBC, ABC, and BBC Television. My story about Rob and his addiction now has been covered by Chinese TV, Japanese, Russian, Netherlands, Denmark, Germany, Holland, Swedish, Korean, Europe including Sky News, and Britannia TV. All those networks came to my house in Owego with news crews to cover my change of heart for my hero who had now fallen from grace in my eyes. I was on the front page of the *Washington Post*, *USA Today*, the *New York Times*, and who knows how many local papers. I was being called by everybody I knew from around the country. "Hey, Moss, did you know you were on the front page of the Tampa newspapers?" Or the *Fresno Bee* or wherever.

As each news outlet contacted me, I told them all the same thing: "He lied to me." That's basically what it boiled down to. They all put a slightly different angle on it, but the message was the same—the Trump Troubadour, the singing cowboy who had so earnestly dedicated months of his life to the election of Donald Trump, now felt disappointed and betrayed. I think the media especially liked the story because it was basically an "I told you so" to the Trump supporters. The other side had warned everyone that he was not truthful and couldn't be trusted. So when they got wind of supporters with a change of heart, they jumped on it like flies on shit.

I didn't mind because they had a point. Trump had promised me, in honor of my son, that he would be fighting the heroin epidemic and look what happened. He tried so hard to push a healthcare bill through that actually took away from the very things he said he would improve. Fortunately, it didn't make it through, but that was his fault as well because he didn't want to work with everyone to come up with a bill that was better than Obamacare, not worse than. President Trump has been promoting his own agendas and whatever he promised the American people doesn't seem to matter anymore. At least that's the way I see it. It's all about Trump and his rich friends and what he can do for them while he's in office. I'm sure the imminent domain issue will go through so as to clear the way for more development that somehow will benefit Trump down the road. Back when I was campaigning in Albuquerque, a Mexican TV station had interviewed me about Rob and why I so passionately supported then-candidate Trump. This whole "in honor of your son" angle really has me so mad because it's as if Rob has become a political bargaining chip. Rob deserves more than a broken promise.

Earlier in 2016, I was flown to Washington, D.C., for a Paul Ryan Town Hall meeting moderated by CNN. They wanted me to be one of the guests who would ask Paul Ryan a question. I didn't like the format. I was told to write down a question, so I did. They rewrote my question and instructed me a half hour before airtime to memorize the wording as they had written it. I don't know whose idea that was, but I didn't like it and neither did the other guests. Everyone was getting nervous trying to memorize the lines to their own damn question! I wanted to confront Paul Ryan and ask him if President Trump even knew what was in the newly proposed healthcare bill. I wanted to ask him if the president knew the contents of the bill and if he was aware that it didn't include anything he promised the American people. I wanted to say that you, Paul Ryan, should be ashamed of yourself. Not only that, the president of the United States, Donald Trump, should be ashamed of himself if both of you know that this proposed healthcare bill doesn't include anything that President Trump promised the American people. It seemed that the only important aspect of it was that it was designed to replace Obamacare. That seemed to be the driving force for ramming the bill through. Shame on you and shame on President Trump!

There were so many things I wanted to discuss with Paul Ryan about his sad little healthcare bill that he seemed so proud and eager to discuss. Was he so anxious to get the bill passed because he had written it? The question I was limited to asking was, "Does this bill mandate doctors to prescribe a detox period where patients would be mandated to participate in a step-down program to ween them off pain killers when prescribed?"

When I finally got to ask the prepared question, he responded that it suggests doctors do this, but that there is no mandate. I did let him know this is the problem. The doctors prescribing these drugs must be held accountable and mandated to educate their patients and require them to offer alternative pain relief before setting them up with a thirty-day supply of something like OxyContin.

What I actually wanted to do was educate people about what is going on in this country. For some reason, most people seem oblivious until it happens to someone they know. According to the Centers for Disease Control and Prevention, opioids—which includes prescription drugs, heroin, and fentanyl—killed over thirty-three thousand US citizens in 2015, which was more than any other year before that. It's also important to note that almost half of all opioid deaths are a result of prescription drugs. That means this horrible addiction impacts everyone, from the underprivileged people getting hooked on street drugs laced with fentanyl to financially stable middle-class suburbanites who are prescribed a powerful and addictive opioid that they cannot escape from. These people become prisoners of their addiction and they feel scared and hopeless. As a country, we have to do better.

During my interviews with other news media, I often touched on the other issues Trump campaigned on such as better healthcare programs for our veterans. Trump promised he would make big changes and promised veterans would be able to use their VA card to receive medical treatment from any medical facility of their choice. He talked about how illegal immigrants who have a welfare card can go to the local hospital or healthcare specialist. Any doctor "illegals" wanted to see is covered by the welfare card, but the man who enlisted and promised to give his life if need be to protect our country has to drive sometimes hundreds of miles to the nearest VA hospital only to be told now and again that his or her appointment was canceled and to come back on another day. The networks I visited never aired that part of my interviews. They only seemed to be interested in all the lies regarding healthcare and the heroin epidemic.

For now, I'm just playing with my band at a benefit here or there to help the Trinity CASA in Owego, New York. We raised $3,100 on that cold night in March and continue to schedule concerts bringing awareness to the heroin epidemic and keeping Rob's memory alive by telling his story to anyone who will listen. I was contacted recently by a man who believes in what I am doing and has offered his assistance in organizing a group for parents who have lost a loved one to opiates. It's a club I never intended to belong to, but somehow, I am now the spokesman.

Though Trump announced some time ago that he was declaring a national emergency in regard to the opiate crises, he hasn't yet approved funding. Anything done without proper funding is useless. The healthcare bill was supposed to include provisions for treatment of addiction, but that wasn't in the plans that I saw. I have to say that even if somehow President Trump manages to get some kind of significant program in place, the damage has already been done. He has shown his hand and has, with no uncertainty, shown the American people he is perfectly capable of looking you in the eye, promising you one thing, and doing the complete opposite. Donald J. Trump is without question every bit the politician he says he's not. He has told the American people what they wanted to hear to get their votes. Not one time has anyone reached out to me from the Trump camp and asked why I am disappointed. I suppose they well know their boss pulled the biggest scam in American history with the rewards of being president and reaching out to his wealthy friends and offering tax cuts and big breaks on corporate expansion. I have to admit the stock market is doing extremely well with no end in sight, but that doesn't really help folks like me.

I would love to be proven wrong. I would be ecstatic if instead of declaring a national crisis or creating a task force, Trump dedicated an actual budget to fighting the opioid crisis in this country. Until that day, I unfortunately can no longer be a Trump supporter. The Trump Troubadour is no more, as they say. I have returned to my job and am working hard to set up benefits for nonprofit organizations and churches that reach out to the addicted. It's the only way I have to contribute, and it gives me purpose. We all need something to motivate us, to give us a reason to get up in the morning. It has to be something other than making money to pay a light or water bill.

I lost everything when I lost my son Rob, including the will to live if I'm being honest. Without him and with my president turning his back on me, it feels like I just can't catch a break. I'm not suicidal by any means because I see that as a very selfish thing to do. However, recently another of my friends passed away. Lyle was a great pal and an honest man. We had known each other since we were little kids. I actually missed his passing because I was campaigning in Ohio when he died and couldn't even attend his funeral. It seems like death has become so commonplace that I'm numb to its effects anymore. I have been hardened by the frequency of it all and the helplessness that I feel. It seems that no matter how much I try, I can't make a difference. Hell, I even dedicated my life to getting someone elected to the highest office in the land and even that didn't go the way I had expected. I will still help those with addiction issues as best I can. One of the TV networks that covered my story after Trump betrayed me went out to Colorado and did a little documentary on a recovering addict. He was so excited to have a three-man crew fly to Denver just to document his life and his struggle kicking his heroin addiction. It gave him hope that someone truly cared.

Two weeks after Rob died, his best friend passed away from a heroin overdose. In 2014, over thirty kids died in Tioga County from heroin overdoses. I have heard that in some jurisdictions, the local police department and EMS often label the heroin deaths as heart failure. I don't know if that's to mask the extent of the issue, but that's what one official told me in confidence. It's truly such a shame that people want to look the other way or stick their head in the sand when it comes to the heroin problem in this country.

Creating a band and playing around the United States serves two purposes—it gives me that motivation to keep going and it helps to spread Rob's cautionary tale to more and more people. I use many of the things I've learned during my time on the Trump Trail. I learned how to get people engaged and motivated to take action. Like I said before, things happen for a reason. Maybe all of that time spent campaigning for Trump wasn't a waste after all. Maybe that was a way to show me how I can get Rob's message across on my own, without empty promises from politicians.

However, I'm not totally on my own. I've assembled a great band to help. We have a pianist who lives in Seattle, Washington, who has played on stage with Billy Joel and many others. Our saxophone player used to play with Three Dog Night, and our cool drummer who lives in Rochester has played with bands across the country. With these guys by my side, I think we can do some good by providing honest entertainment with a message that everyone needs to hear. Just like people didn't believe Trump would win, a lot of folks don't want to believe there's a serious drug problem, but it can't be ignored any longer. It's a fact and we have to deal with it. Young, old, rich, poor, black, white—it's a problem that we must all come together to conquer.

I thought there was a sign of hope when Trump announced in October 2017 plans to establish yet another opioid task force and appoint a new "drug czar." Then the first selection for the appointment, Representative Tom Marino from Pennsylvania, withdrew his name from the selection process after a report surfaced indicating he had taken around $100,000 from a pharmaceutical lobby interest in support of a bill he had sponsored that would actually allow drug companies to circumvent the Drug Enforcement Agency and more easily distribute opioids to the public.

That just reinforced my belief that there is no truth to any of this. It's all rhetoric and machinations that amount to nothing. An issue this serious should not be treated so lightly. Where is the vetting process? Where is the due diligence? I'm sure there will be more announcements in the weeks and months to come. Task forces will be created and likely never heard from again. Drug czars will come and go, changing little and acquiring a new line item on their political resume.

I really thought things would be different with this man. He really spoke to me in the beginning. He did what no one else could do—he mobilized me and millions like me who never took an interest in politics. We saw in him a new beginning, a man who would stand up for us.

In the end, all we got was another politician who couldn't (or wouldn't) tell the truth.

Here I am with a box of ashes by my side to talk to every day when I get up and every night before I go to bed. I feel Rob's presence and just wish things had turned out differently. I'm back in Ohio working the gas fields once again. Not a day goes by that I don't think about my son. Sometimes I just can't help feeling like I let my son down, and then I was let down again by the man I helped to get elected.

I was let down by Donald Trump.

ACKNOWLEDGMENTS

I have so many people to thank—who at some point were supportive of me when I was a child, or when I was in the working world by giving me strength by patting me on the back and saying "good job," or later in life from those I've come to know on the Trump Trail who helped me when I was down or those I work with every day. Also those whom I have shared time with. The following is a brief list of people I would like to thank for helping me at some point in my life. Special thank-you to the following:

Jo-an Pinter Moss, my first love from grade school and my third wife. I thank you for keeping me in your thoughts and talking to me when I've been down. Although our attempt at marriage didn't work, we both know what could have been. Thank you for being you and being there for me when I needed a friend.

Brandy and Seth Ravert have been so supportive of me on the Trump Trail, even though we didn't share the same feelings about our beloved president.

Jordan Marsh, for forgiving me for some harsh words shared along the way.

Richard and Gloria Tubbs, who believed in me so much that they sent me money when I was stranded on the Trump Trail and they didn't even know me. The Trump campaign wouldn't send me gas money, but you folks sure did.

ACKNOWLEDGMENTS

Cindy French, Barney French, and our mutual friend Madaline, who would ask me to come up on the hill when I'm in town and called me when I was on the road just to check up on me. Forever friends.

Mike Krems from St. Louis, who met me at the RNC and took me to the Rock and Roll Hall of Fame. He also took the trip to my neck of the woods in New York and was master of ceremonies at the sixth Rob Moss Heroin Awareness Tour.

Diane Nine, of Nine Speakers, who is my very hard-working literary agent. You believed in me and gave me the courage to write this all down.

Rowman & Littlefield, I thank you for taking me under your wing and giving me a chance. Without your support, I'm not sure where I'd be, if anywhere at all.

Dave Smitherman, you are such a brilliant and clever writer. I have been honored to have worked with you and truly enjoyed our interactions throughout these writings. Thank you.

Larry and Char England—well, you folks just continue to bless me with your friendship. Maybe someday I might take you up on your offer and come serve the Lord with you at your cowboy church in Iowa. I thank you for all your hospitality while I was on the Trump Trail.

Morning Star Cowboy Church, for always having your doors open for me to receive the Word. Everyone there just gets a big hug from me and I hope to see y'all soon.

Roger Steen, my goodness, where would I ever start? From believing in me in the 1980s and giving me a job, to being there for me when I needed something. Nobody else could deliver the truth about losing a son. I'm sorry you're in this club with me, but your honest insight really prepared me for the brutal truth: The pain never goes away. It may go dormant, but it never goes away. Those who told me to give it time have no clue. You've been a friend to me through some hard times, and those times you helped me stay on the Trump Trail when you were struggling yourself really have sunk in to my heart, where I will have a place for you, forever.

Thank you, Deb, for the phone call now and again for support.

All those struggling addicts who called me and let me know my efforts have been appreciated and I'm doing Rob proud by standing up for the addicted folks who can't stand up for themselves. Your communications have been very welcome, and I thank you all.

ACKNOWLEDGMENTS

My family—it feels so good to say "my family"—Uncle Erik, Aunt Chris, Uncle Bud, and Aunt Lisa, along with all my cousins. You have provided me with a warm family environment even if for such a brief time during a holiday now and again. Uncle Erik, you and Chris have reminded me how strong the Lord's Word is and how important it is to not lose faith. Never lose faith in my Lord and Savior, Jesus Christ.

My sister for her continued love and support.

Ron Hills for being a friend and counseling me throughout the campaign.

Bonnie and Doug, well, just plain thanks for being there when I needed to talk to someone on the Trump Trail. I am so grateful to the whole crew at the cabin who helped raise over $3,000 for the organization in Owego that helps struggling addicts.

Thank you, Jason and Kelly, for your continued friendship.

Special thanks to a special lady. Thank you, Pam, for helping me keep focused and offering your support. You have truly been a blessing.

Mrs. Myers, for picking up my mail and watching my house when I was on the Trump Trail.

And last but not least, thanks to all the people who reached out to me at the rallies. You know who you are. All of you who spoke to me, listened to me talk about my son, and shared concern about the heroin epidemic, especially those who experienced similar tragedies in their own life from drug addiction. I was so touched when many of you appeared from the crowd and just spilled your emotions to me about the loss of a son or daughter. You see, it's those interactions and your talks to me that made my following Mr. Trump around the country worthwhile. If nothing else good ever happens with this presidency, you have all touched me so dearly and I will forever be grateful for your kindness.

Thanks to Ron at Ronald Evans Photography in Binghamton, New York, for the great photographs. Visit his Facebook page: https://www.facebook.com/RonaldEvansPhotography/.

Finally, thanks to the talented painting preacher who invited me to Iowa and started me on the Trump Trail. He also demonstrated prayer every day.

God Bless You All.

INDEX

Note: The photo insert images between pages 74 and 75 are indexed as *p1, p2, p3*, etc.

75–76, 117, 118; stepchildren and, 67–68, 69; struggles with single, 123
fathers: abuse from, 20, 29; alcoholism of, 19–20, 21, 22–23; death of, 13, 29–30; disappointment from, 20, 24, 29, 117, 130; drug addiction blame on, 83, 108
father-son relationship: activities central to, 123–24, 128, 130; anger and fighting in, 29, 137, 143; love in, 29–30, 92; with Moss, R., *p2*, *p4*, 4–5, *p5*, *p6*, 11, 102–3, 119–20, 123–24, 128–30, 137–38, 143–44
Fayetteville, North Carolina, 81, 82
fentanyl, 49, 85, 95, 114, 144, 153
fighting. *See* anger and fighting
financial management, 44; drug use impact on, 58, 64; for music production, 98; teaching Moss, R., about, 5; on Trump Trail, 17, 40–41, 43, 46, 48, 50, 95–96, 112–13
Financial Times, 84
Finland, 25
fishing, 128, 130
Florida, 9, 83–87, 111
foreign journalists/media: interviews with, 42, 52–53, 151; Trump, D., restriction of, 53; on Trump Trail, 32, 42, 52–53, 85
foreign policy, 132
Forrest, Steve, 151
Fort Conrad, Indiana, 102–3
foster care, 117–18
420, 97
Fox News, 42, 44, 151
friends, 4, 26; death of, 14, 155; grief aided by, 13–14, 93; negative influence of, 8, 142–45; truck driving, 62–64; on Trump Trail,

33–34, 38–40, 49, 50, 82–83, 112–13
fundraising: at church, 104–105, 106, 111; for drug treatment, 154; for Trump Trail, 47–48, 53; for veterans, 44
funerals, 14

gas and oil industry, 80
generosity: at church, 104–5; of supporters, 39–40, 41, 111–13
"Gonna Build a Wall" (song), 94, 98, 108
GQ Magazine, 33
Graham, Billy, 30
grandparents, 24–28, 114, 124–25
grief: Cowboy Church support for, 47–48; friends help with, 13–14, 93; around holidays, 93–94; longevity of, 4, 14–15, 90–93, 145, 155; prayer in, 90; rallies as catharsis for, 53–54; shared on Trump Trail, 49, 97; upon suicide note discovery, 91–93, 102–3
guns, 78, 125–26

Hagerstown, Maryland, 94–95
healthcare: Clinton on, 131; supporters focus on, 148, 149; Trump, D., in-office actions on, 150–51, 153, 156; Trump, D., promises on, 31, 102, 151; for veterans, 153–54
heroin: addiction, 6–7, 12, 83, 140–42, 149–50; awareness techniques, 155–56; drug overdose from, 12–13, 16–17, 37, 49, 80–81, 94–95, 144; fentanyl combined with, 49, 85, 95, 114, 144; music for awareness about, 150, 154, 156; smoking,

rural environment: in childhood, 19,
25–28; drugs in, 6; peace in, 39, 104
Russia, 149
Ryan, Paul, 152–53

Sanders, Bernie, 89–90, 99
San Jose, California, 111
Secret Service, 36, 37–38, 78–79, 95
selfishness, 117–18
semi-trucks. *See* truck driving
siblings, 23–24, 28, 129. *See also* sister
Sioux Center, Iowa, 39–40, 75
sister, 19, 23–24, 28, 87–88
skiing, 23, 24
smoking. *See* cigarette smoking
South Bend, Indiana, 103
South Carolina, 48–53, 76, 85
sports, 23, 24
stepchildren: bonding with, 67–68, 69;
connection after divorce with, 101–2
stepmothers, *p7*, 120–23
St. Louis, Missouri, 82–83, 88
suicide: of friends, 141–42; Moss, R.,
note indicating, 91–92, 96–97,
102–3
Super Tuesday, 76, 79–80
supporters, 1–2, 15; on aggressive
behavior, 44; attention-seeking of,
41, 42, 46; Campaign Headquarters
enlisting/funding, 43, 50; cigarette
smoking of, 77; commonalities
of, 33, 38, 49, 51, 80, 85–86, 95;
disappointment after inauguration
of, 148–57; with drug addiction,
81, 83; financial gain agenda for,
51; focus and reasonings for, 133,
148, 149; generosity of, 39–40, 41,
112; on Mexico and immigrants,
78, 108, 109; passion of, 75; polls
compared to experience for, 133–34;

protester conflict with, 82, 103,
108–9; protesters celebrating with,
115; religion and, 16, 18, 34, 38, 78;
songs on Trump Trail reception by,
42, 87; Trump Trail increase of, 37,
38, 45
Swedish heritage and language, 25, 26,
27, 52
Swedish media/journalists, 52, 53,
85, 151

Tapper, Jake, 151
tax cuts, 154
teeter-totters, 28
Tennessee, 81
Toledo, Ohio, 114
tractors, 26, 28
treatment programs, 122, 150, 154
tree cutting, 70–71
Trinity CASA, 149–50, 154
truck driving, 1, 11; death from drug
use while, 63; drug use while, 59,
62–63; exhaustion while, 62–64;
friendships while, 62–64; love
relationship found while, 55–61;
skills on Trump Trail, 32
truck stops, 55–56
Trump, Donald: aggressive behavior
of, 44, 80; attention-seeking nature
of, 35–36, 80, 148–49; conflict
with issues supported by, 118, 131,
148–57; deportation policy of, 56,
147; on foreign media at rallies,
53; free advertising technique of,
35; gratitude from, 115; healthcare
and drug policy actions by, 150–51,
153, 156; healthcare promises
made by, 31, 102, 151; Indiana
success for, 103; Iowa caucuses loss
for, 45; on media and journalists,

ABOUT THE AUTHOR

Kraig Moss was dubbed "The Trump Troubadour" after he dressed in western wear and traveled the country performing his music at Trump rallies and discussing the horrible heroin and opioid epidemic in this country.

Learn more by visiting: http://www.trumptroubadour.com/.